Mozart the Freemason

Mozart the Freemason

The Masonic Influence on His Musical Genius

Jacques Henry

FOREWORD BY BRIGITTE MASSIN

*Translated from the French
by Jack Cain*

Inner Traditions
Rochester, Vermont

Inner Traditions
One Park Street
Rochester, Vermont 05767
www.InnerTraditions.com

Originally published in French in 1991 by Éditions ALINÉA and in 1997
by Éditions du Rocher under the title *Mozart Frère Maçon: La symbolique
maçonnique dans l'oeuvre de Mozart*
First U.S. Edition published in 2006 by Inner Traditions

Library of Congress Cataloging-in-Publication Data
Henry, Jacques.
  [Mozart frère maçon. English]
  Mozart the freemason : the masonic influence on his musical genius / Jacques
Henry ; translated from the French by Jack Cain ; foreword by Brigitte Massin.
     p. cm.
  Originally published: Aix-en-Provence : Alinéa, c1991.
  Includes bibliographical references and index.
  ISBN-13: 978-1-59477-128-6 (pbk.)
  ISBN-10: 1-59477-128-6 (pbk.)
  1. Mozart, Wolfgang Amadeus, 1756-1791—Freemasonry. I. Cain, Jack,
1940- trl II. Massin, Brigitte. III. Title.
  ML410.M9.H312 2006
  780.92—dc22

                                                                    2006016307

Printed and bound in the United States by Lake Book Manufacturing

10 9 8 7 6 5 4 3 2 1

Text design and layout by Rachel Goldenberg
This book was typeset in Sabon with Bickham Script Pro as the display typeface

To L. H. and P. L.

Contents

Foreword

Why this book? Well, there's a story behind it. A short time ago, when I made the acquaintance of Jacques Henry, the purpose of our meeting was Mozart and preparations for the composer's bicentenary celebrations. Jacques wanted to be familiar with large projects related to this event in order to assess which of them he might be able to carry out himself.

He spoke to me then of his passion and love for Mozart, beginning at age fourteen and never abandoned as he grew up; his familiarity with Mozart's works and their companionship with him in the various places he has lived and worked—Switzerland, Argentina, Canada, Africa, France; and his in-depth research in order to come closer to the personality of Mozart as an individual. And in concluding, he confided to me, in a voice of the most straightforward simplicity and directness:

"This is why I entered freemasonry myself at the age of about forty—in order to share in the same vision that freemasonry had opened for Mozart, in order to live this same conviction and to be capable of fully grasping the connection between musical expression and the substance of initiation."

I found this approach striking and impressive in its forthrightness. At the end of the interview, I asked whether he would accept conveying in a book the results of his reflections and his research on Mozart without separating them from the direction of his own approach.

Much has already been written and published on Mozart and the freemasonry of his era. These works are scholarly and the result of careful research. They are often the work of musicologists or historians. Their propositions have been widely discussed and their assertions debated, to everyone's great benefit. But this is probably the first time that a freemason has spoken openly about what an initiation has revealed to him, just as the same initiation would have revealed it to Mozart.

Previous research on this subject has often moved from the externals of freemasonry into its more internal aspects, such as its history and symbolism. Here the method is just the opposite. From inside the lodge the author tries, for himself and the layman, to highlight the similarities between what he has to say and what Mozart drew from freemasonry as he lived it. In other words, Jacques raises the question of the relationship between symbol and inspiration, the content of the symbol forming in his eyes the very source of inspiration.

In freemasonry there are many diverse currents and allegiances that for historical, ideological, or philosophical reasons do not adopt the same view of the world, nor the manner of understanding the role of freemasonry in our society.

Jacques Henry's readers will quickly realize that he belongs to a current that he himself describes as "spiritualist and regularly traditional." Moreover, the author is determined to follow across the centuries the same initiatory and ontological dimension that inspired Mozart, in order to share it with the reader.

The elevation of Jacques' perspective characterizes this work—the serene view that he brings to the study of Mozart's repertoire. In addition, the quality of the personal research of a Mozart devotee, the clarity of his writing, and the pertinence of his new insights open us to the depth of Mozart's engagement with his art and show us another facet of his inspiration. That is what Jacques helps us to see, writing with a quiet forthrightness as one who has wished to follow in Mozart's footsteps in order to proceed further in the understanding of his art.

Here a freemason speaks to the layman as well as to his brothers. We must follow him on this road to knowledge, and as we do so, Mozart's path will be more brightly lit and Mozart will become not only closer to us, but a brother.

Brigitte Massin

Brigitte Massin was a musicologist who specialized in the works of Beethoven, Schubert, and Mozart. She wrote *Guide des opéras de Mozart, La Petite encyclopédie de la musique, Les Joaquim: Une famille de musicians,* and *Wolfgang Amadeus Mozart* (with her husband, Jean Massin).

Preface

Mozart was not only the cherished child of the gods, composing music for the greatest joy of the angels; he was also the man who died murmuring the notes of a fragmentary "Lacrymosa" for his unfinished Requiem: tears that the world was henceforth obliged to shed in expiation for having let the greatest genius of music die in darkest misery. Research based on recently discovered and published documents has had the particular merit of ascribing to Mozart a personality closer to what he must have had in reality and delineating the profound influence of freemasonry on the final years of his life and work.

A fact brought out by Carl de Nys struck my attention: the fusion during the last ten years of Mozart's life between his original faith in God—a religious and Christian faith—and his Masonic faith in the Great Architect of the Universe.[1] I was amazed to realize that there was no difference in inspiration between the last Masonic cantata (K. 623) and the Requiem (K. 626); to me, both works seem to lead equally, by means of different musical expressions, to an identical vision of the Beyond, a vision that Mozart reached at the end of his life.

Some authors tend to look for Masonic inspiration in Mozart's compositions where in fact there is none. Others engage in dissecting the compositions in order to discover symbols or allusions that Mozart definitely did not put there. And still others, displaying anti-Masonic sentiment, denounce all conclusions that are reached by research conducted with the sole aim of expressing a truth.

I understood that in order to rigorously evaluate the influence of Masonic symbolism, it would be necessary to study it not from the outside but to live it in its context within the fraternity and above all to practice the rite and its ceremonies. I wanted to become Mozart's Masonic brother across the centuries, to live today what he himself lived in the Lodge, to practice a ritual that has remained in its entirety the same since his time. My aim was to understand the symbolism, to analyze and perceive the initiatory value of these same symbols, to follow the same philosophical research, and to try to reach the light as he himself was able to do. An analysis of Masonic symbolism that is not founded on what has been lived is by no means capable of grasping what constitutes the very rationale of his composition.

Therefore, this study has but one aim: to analyze as rigorously as possible the exact role of symbolism, insofar as it is a true musical language in Mozart's creation and its power of inspiration. In order to do this, it is necessary to refrain from using words that would only be understood by an enlightened minority. A limiting analysis of what Mozart wanted understood by everyone would be a serious mistake.

Following other writers who have subtly expressed the same point, we have come to recognize that Mozart's great works are clearly inspired by a symbolism that bestows on them a universal grandeur. Such great compositions are not to be found on the (unfortunately very restricted) record that for a long time has classified certain works as Masonic and which we will henceforth call the List (Appendix 1, p. 123).

Since the influence of Masonic symbolism on Mozart's work is the sole purpose of this study, we will not analyze the compositions in this official List unless they are of interest, or Mozart found it necessary to reuse the content of such works proceeding from the same Masonic inspiration. This is particularly the case with the Adagio in B flat major (K. 411) that has been integrated in an almost identical form into the second movement of Concerto No. 22 for piano in E flat major (K. 482).

For personal reasons and on very specific occasions between 1785 and his death, Mozart had recourse to a musical language that transcribed Masonic symbols so that his work, through its harmony, would express their profound value. This musical language is not unique to Mozart, but it is he who raised it to its highest level of expression "in a manner that was genial and impossible to ascribe to anyone else."[2]

Part 1

Mozart and the Masonic Enlightenment

1

Mozart, Masonic Brother

The importance of freemasonry in the eighteenth century is difficult to imagine today: all the more so since its nineteenth-century adversaries' portrait of it is still very much present. Among the currents of thought of the period, freemasonry stands out as one that has most deeply influenced intellectual society. In Mozart's time, the Masonic order assembled everything that Europe considered brilliant. Thinkers and artists fully supported the great principle of Masonic thought (also called the Royal Art): the betterment of man through the respect and observance of ideals of a rigorous morality. This vision of the world and humanity went hand in hand with the philosophical movement that touched all of Europe and made of the eighteenth century the Age of Enlightenment (*die Aufklärung; l'Éclairecissement*).

The Masonic Order, which declared itself to be officially religious and outwardly professed its belief in God or, more precisely, its belief in the Great Architect of the Universe, left to individuals the choice of belonging to whichever church they wished. (The papacy could not tolerate this freedom of belief and condemned the Order with a papal bull in 1738.)

Major writers such as Schiller, Goethe, and Lessing openly developed in their works the principles that had been revealed to them through their adherence to freemasonry. High-level personages in Germany and Austria belonged to the Order: the Emperor Francis himself, the Austrian statesman Prince Wenzel Anton Kaunitz, Baron Otto von Gemmingen, Ignaz von Born (Grand Master of the United Lodges), Joseph von Sonnenfels (a law professor and advisor to Empress Maria Theresa), and Baron Gottfried van Swieten (a patron of Mozart and Beethoven as well as a collaborator with Joseph Haydn)—the last three most strongly influencing Mozart's life in freemasonry up to his final hours.

Numerous musicians also attended the Lodges, which explains the importance of music in the ceremonies. Roger Cotte, in writing about such Parisian Lodges as "l'Harmonie," "l'Olympique," and "les Amis Réunis," mentions, among others, Nicolas Dalayrac, André Danican Philidor, Niccolò Piccini, Luigi Cherubini, Etienne Nicholas Méhul, Giroud, François-Joseph Gossec, André-Ernest-Modeste Grétry, and François Devienne.[1]

In Vienna, Mozart associated with musicians such as the tenor Johann Adamberger and especially the Stadler brothers, clarinetists for whom he composed works with Masonic influences (works that we will return to later). He was on friendly terms with Joseph Haydn, whose initiation to freemasonry he sponsored. He worked with Emanuel Schikaneder in the composition of *The Magic Flute* and the Masonic Cantata "In Praise of Friendship" (K. 623). And it should be mentioned that when he needed support in moments of great material difficulty or low morale, he would always turn to his Masonic brother, the merchant Michael Puchberg.

Jacques Chailley, basing his work on the freemason Serge Hutin's book *Les Franc-Maçons,* outlines the vast scope that freemasonry enjoyed in Vienna in the middle of the eighteenth century. [2] A few significant numbers from Chailley's work need to be repeated here. After its foundation in London in 1717, freemasonry continued to develop without interruption. In France for example, there were 30,000 brothers in 1776 and 70,000 in 1787. The Great Lodge of Austria, founded in 1742, comprised sixty-two Lodges at the time of Mozart's initiation, including eight in Vienna alone.

The evolution of the attitude of Emperor Joseph II toward freemasonry to some extent shaped Austria's history. In 1738, Pope Clement XII issued a papal bull condemning the Masonic order. However, papal edicts, in order to be officially recognized and applied, had to be promulgated by the Austrian civil authorities. Emperor Francis, who had himself been initiated in May 1731, did not issue the promulgation decree. We can assume that he was influenced by his son, the future Joseph II, who during his reign (1765–1790) had no wish to issue this kind of condemnation. This tolerance can be explained by sympathy and respect for Masonic ideas and the desire to protect the highest figures of the regime who belonged to the Order.

In January 1786, Mozart composed two songs for the inauguration of the new Lodge "New Hope Crowned": one to welcome a visitor and the other to accompany his departure. These two songs, "Today Be Moved, Dear Brothers" (K. 483), and "To You, Our Leaders New" (K. 484), portray simple ideas of morality; more importantly they are in honor of Joseph II. Mozart composed the cantata "Die Maurerfreude" ("The Mason's Joy"), K. 471 to be sung by Johann Valentin Adamberger; Mozart directed the performance on April 24, 1785, during a ritual ceremony for a special dinner. It praises the Emperor: "Sing brothers for the wise Joseph has crowned the Masonic Temple with laurel."

The Emperor's stance had a considerable influence on Austrian Catholicism because belonging to the Order entailed no ecclesiastical dilemma for a Catholic. Besides, numerous representatives of the clergy and even prelates belonged to lodges. This situation was very convenient for a large number of Catholics who were not inclined toward religious practice and who were scarcely respectful of clerical authority. They were much more inclined to believe in the ascendancy of reason and brotherhood, both of which were ideals promoted by *Aufklärung* and freemasonry. The Catholic freemason in Austria was therefore an "enlightened Catholic." There is no doubt that this was the attitude of both Mozart and his father Leopold.

Although Joseph II was never really opposed to freemasonry, in which he found support and justification for his politics of enlightened despotism, he nevertheless decided to reorganize its administrative structure in order to ensure, with the help of trusted friends, control over the organization. More and more, it had gained an influence and importance within the structures of the state that the Emperor could not tolerate. As the years went by, authorities perceived the philosophical framework of freemasonry as harboring new ideas and, above all, as dangerous because they considered it revolutionary.

On December 11, 1785, the Emperor issued a decree requiring the amalgamation of the eight Lodges of Vienna into only three. This change was implemented at the beginning of 1786.

The Lodge where Mozart was initiated, Zur Wohltätigkeit ("Charity"), one of the smallest in the city, was amalgamated with the most important, Zur Gekrönten Hoffnung ("Hope Crowned") and Zur den drei Feuern ("The Three Fires") to become Zur Neugekrönten Hoffnung ("New Hope Crowned," or as it is often wrongly translated, "Hope Newly Crowned") on January 14, 1787. Contrary to what one might have thought, Mozart did not change lodges in the course of his life in freemasonry.

A new lodge, Die Wahrheit ("Truth"), established January 6, 1786, amalgamated three others: Zum Palmbaum ("The Palm"); Zu den drei Adlern ("The Three Eagles"); and the most important, Zur Wahren Eintracht ("True Harmony"), whose Grand Master Ignaz von Born was the organizer of the amalgamation. It should be mentioned in this regard that the brothers of True Harmony added their support to that of Charity for Mozart's initiation (see Appendix 2). Wolfgang attended von Born's Lodge as often as his own mother Lodge. We know that he was present at the assemblies of January 7, 14, and 28, February 11, and April 16, 1785. This was also the Lodge where Mozart had Joseph Haydn initiated in February 1785, as well as his father, who was visiting Vienna in March 1785.

Two other lodges, Zum Heiligen Joseph ("To St. Joseph") and Zur Beständigkeit ("Steadfastness"), were closed and certain of their brothers joined the two remaining reorganized Lodges.

Joseph II died on February 20, 1790. His brother Leopold II succeeded him. At this time, the French Revolution had been proceeding for several months and Marie-Antoinette, the wife of Louis XVI, was the Emperor's sister. This is why, even if Leopold did not explicitly condemn freemasonry, he brought it under close and rigorous surveillance.

The issue of secret societies was complex. Two other orders existed alongside official freemasonry. The first of these, "The

Enlightened Ones of Bavaria," was founded in 1776 by Professor Adam Weishaupt. This order was completely separate from free-masonry but freemasons subsequently joined it.

Weishaupt had been initiated in the "Strict Observance," the second independent order. The unfortunate stir created by these two orders compromised official freemasonry through the practice of cross-memberships. Leopold Mozart, already an initiate, wrote to his daughter on October 14, 1785: "I have learned that one percent of what is said here (in Salzburg) about the 'Enlightened Ones of Munich' is true. . . . According to what I'm told by the oboist Ramm, authentic freemasons (who include the Elector of Bavaria) are very annoyed by these strange gentlemen." Historians believe that Mozart and his father, before their initiation, could have belonged to these movements. We don't think so. They both associated with members of the order of "Enlightened Ones," but their relationships were limited to personal friendships.

Such suspicions held by zealous detractors, based nevertheless on a few facts, led Leopold II to decree certain severe personal measures concerning high officials. Baron Gottfried van Swieten, for example, who had remained Mozart's friend and protector, received a notice relieving him of all his official duties on December 5, 1791 (notably, the day of Wolfgang's death). It is presumed that this was linked to a Masonic conspiracy.[3] This sanction certainly must have troubled van Swieten and is the reason he was unable, during this pain and hardship, to give his brother's widow Constanze the full extent of fraternal support that he wished for her.

Mozart lived through this difficult period of the decline of Austrian freemasonry that followed the restructuring. However, from the day of his initiation forward, he remained deeply convinced of the philosophic and moral value of freemasonry. He regretted that political contingencies could have altered his ideal in the public's eyes. This is why, with *The Magic Flute*, he proved himself to be an ardent defender of Masonic initiation and its universal message.

Mozart's membership in freemasonry was not an impulsive act; nor, above all, did it turn into a superficial gesture as was the case with Haydn. In the course of the last seven years of his life, Mozart could have forgotten its importance little by little, as Haydn did. This was absolutely not the case. Mozart found in the Royal Art what he had been seeking more or less consciously for a long time.

Well before December 1784, Mozart often had occasion to come into contact with Masonic thought and ideals and to meet in his travels influential masons, certain of whom would later become brothers. When he was eleven years old, Wolfgang apparently had his first contact with freemasonry, a trace of which has survived. He thanked Dr. Wolff of Olmütz, who had cured him of smallpox, by setting to music an arietta by J. P. Uz, "An die Freude" ("To Joy") (K. 53). The choice of this poem is interesting since the words are inspired by Masonic sentiments. The theme of joy, invoked like those of peace and love among men at the end of every assembly, is a fundamental tenet of Masonic thought.

A year later, Mozart met a famous European freemason, Dr. Anton Mesmer, who entrusted him with the musical composition of *Bastien und Bastienne* (K. 50, inspired by the *Devin de Village* by Jean-Jacques Rousseau), a *singspiel* (small opera) that he wanted to have staged at his theatre near Vienna. There is nothing Masonic about the work itself. However, it is noteworthy that the association between Mesmer and the young Wolfgang left traces in the boy's thought. In *Così Fan Tutte*, Mozart would later evoke with irony a cure using magnetism, a speciality of Mesmer's that had become fashionable at the time.

In 1773, the freemason Baron Tobias Philippe von Gebler entrusted Mozart with the composition of the stage music for *Thamos, König von Ägypten* (*Thamos, King of Egypt*), the subject of which, as we shall see, was inspired by symbolic themes.

At Mannheim during the final months of 1778 after his return from Paris, he hinted to his father that he was beginning the composition of *Semiramis*, a melodrama inspired by freemasonry—a task that he said he shouldered joyfully. The text, based on a Voltaire play, was by Baron von Gemmingen; it is lost to us today. Gemmingen was a diplomat originally from Mannheim, where Mozart had met him on his way to Paris. The friendship that developed between them was to be a determining factor in Mozart's life. In a letter written to his father on March 24, 1778, Wolfgang mentioned that von Gemmingen had given him a letter recommending him to Count Sickingen, Minister of the Palatinat in Paris. In this same letter, he noted that before his departure he had copies made for Gemmingen of a quartet (K. 80), a quintet (K. 174), and twelve variations (K. 179). Gemmingen left Mannheim for Vienna in 1782. In 1784, Gemmingen, Grand Master of the Charity Lodge, conducted Mozart's initiation and was undoubtedly also Mozart's sponsor.

During the first months following his initiation, Mozart displayed an exceptional zeal. He reached the degree of Fellowcraft on January 7, 1785. The proceedings of the assembly of the "True Harmony" Lodge dated April 22, 1785, suggest that he is already a Master mason because this was an assembly of the third degree. To reach these levels he was obliged, as was the case for all masons who rise in the hierarchy, to present works (usually called "papers"). It is very likely that certain works that he composed in this first trimester of 1785 were recognized and accepted in the Lodge as such. By analyzing them, we will see that some works of this period are indeed very directly influenced by Masonic symbolism and will show how that shaped their inspiration. However, they remain works whose esoteric character must remain hidden to the uninitiated.

Mozart's zeal was not only apparent in the number and richness of his compositions. It also motivated him during the time he led his father toward initiation. Even though, as seen in his correspondence, Leopold seemed to be an enlightened and liberal character, it also appears that he would not have so willingly joined or so rapidly risen in the hierarchy without his son's urging. On April 1, 1785, the Charity Lodge records state that a request was received to conduct Leopold's initiation as quickly as possible given the brevity of his stay in Vienna. On April 6, he was received as Entered Apprentice; on the sixteenth he moved to the degree of Fellowcraft; and on April 22 he was elevated to the degree of Master mason (see Appendix 2). These ceremonies clearly show a reversal of roles: the authoritarian father adopting the ideals of a zealous and especially convincing son.

Under Wolfgang's influence, not only his father but also Joseph Haydn was initiated during the first months of 1785.

We cannot overemphasize the insistent and convincing influence that could impel two personalities of such importance, fame, and fixed ideas to adopt in such a short time the convictions of this young man of twenty-eight.

We know that Haydn was not to remain an ardent freemason, but we also know that in 1786, upon the request of the brother Knight of Saint George, orchestra conductor of the "Olympic"

Lodge in Paris, he offered to that Lodge six symphonies, of which three (numbers 84, 85, and 86) were influenced by Masonic symbolism. We can identify in them, particularly in their introductions, a musical language that is characteristic of Masonic thought. Robbins Landon shows us that Mozart could have learned of these symphonies when Haydn stayed in Vienna in December 1786.[4] Wolfgang would have had them in mind when, in 1788, he composed his last three symphonies; the similarity in inspiration and in writing style is, as Landon points out, especially clear. This similarity is demonstrated by the reappearance in Mozart's works of Masonic symbols already used by Haydn and known to both brothers.

On his return to Salzburg, Leopold Mozart remained an honorary member of his mother lodge in Vienna even though he might no longer have attended assemblies. He seems therefore to have retained his Masonic beliefs. This raises a very serious question and it appears to have been addressed in Wolfgang's famous letter to his sick father on April 4, 1787. "Since death (when we look closely) is the true and final goal of our life, I have, for several years, become so well acquainted with this true and perfect friend of Man, that its image is not only not frightening anymore, but has become very calming, very consoling. And I offer thanks to my God for having afforded me the good fortune of grasping the opportunity (you understand me) of learning to become acquainted with the key of our true happiness."

The phrase "you understand me" indicates not only discretion but also complicity. Mozart's father had remained an initiate and it was to the initiate that Mozart recalled the happiness that was revealed to them by an identical, shared initiation—one that Mozart invoked by using the deliberately neutral term "opportunity." This exchange of correspondence must have continued, even if at a reduced frequency, during the period between the initiation and Leopold's death. Except for this letter, nothing remains of the correspondence of the period from 1785 to 1787; it was apparently destroyed by Wolfgang's widow Constanze, or by those around her. Indeed, if such letters existed, as we have every right to believe they did, they must have referred to freemasonry or freemason friends they had in common. After 1791 it was dangerous to refer to names of masons or mention freemasonry, which, for political reasons, had become suspect. We might regret the destruction of this correspondence, but Constanze believed she was acting wisely.

Mozart was Catholic and remained devout his whole life. His belief in divinity and the Beyond remained alive but underwent an actual substitution; he simply expressed his belief in other forms. After his departure from Salzburg in 1781, religious practice no longer occupied the same place in his life. The only church music written after that year is the Mass in C minor (K. 427), composed for Constanze in 1783. This mass was never finished (as was the case with the Requiem). There is no evidence that Mozart remained a practicing Catholic after settling in Vienna. This was a deliberate break with both the confining and capricious world in which he had grown up and with its accompanying religious practice. But his belief itself was not affected, and God remained alive in Mozart's heart and mind. However, the essential point is that his conception of God changed. The God he invoked and prayed to in youth was replaced by the Architect of the Universe revealed to him in his initiation. For Mozart, the rites and teachings of freemasonry were simply an extension of the rites of the Catholic religion.

However, there was another reason why Mozart was not disappointed by his participation in freemasonry. We know that until his break with his employer Hieronymus Colleredo, Prince-Archbishop of Salzburg, he had to suffer class distinctions that treated him as a servant (the Archbishop's composers were part of his kitchen staff). He had to appear at the time and place the archbishop specified, while his enlightened admirers in the world of the Court would wait expectantly to applaud his music. This social aspect of Mozart's life has perhaps not been sufficiently highlighted. To him, the position he held in Salzburg was humiliating and unjust. It is clear that he suffered more from the financial difficulties of his youth than from those he encountered later, about which we see no sign of outward rebellion. The letters in which he railed against his situation as a despised employee (in particular the correspondence with his father in April 1781) are much more numerous than those in which he deplored his financial difficulties. As painful as these were, they never cast him out of his circle of friends, freemasons or not, to which he belonged through the genius of his mind.

The Masonic brotherhood, an extension of this friendship, also acquainted him with what had always been his aspiration: equality in heart and intelligence. He was an equal to the important personages of the aristocracy whom he met through freemasonry; they afforded him the recognition and dignity that Salzburg and its archbishop had always denied him.

By means of a ritual invocation, freemasons wish "strength and courage in the face of the Eternal Orient" for those about to die. Mozart lived his last moments displaying not only this strength and courage but also complete serenity since, according to those who were present, he seemed to be humming at the same time the "Lacrymosa" from the Requiem and the Papageno theme from *The Magic Flute*.

It is surprising to realize that Mozart wrote his last chord on the word "light": the final word of the Masonic song "Lasst uns mit geschlungen Händen" ("Let us join our hands") (K. 623a), a veritable song of farewell that expresses gratitude to God and wishes for the successful accomplishment of the work to which hearts are devoted. One cannot remain indifferent to the simplicity of this humble song that is so close to the *Ave Verum* (K. 618). Mozart knew that it was appropriate to express a similar serenity in two texts that were similar in their elevation of thought. His last notes mingle with these words whose meaning is only enhanced by the musical harmony: "Venerate virtue and humanity, learn love of self and of others; may this be always our primary duty. And then, not only in the Orient and in the Sunset but also in the South and in the North, Light will stream down."

Certain musicologists doubt the authenticity of this song (K. 623a) since Mozart did not record it in his own hand in the catalogue of his works. But neither is there anything to prove that it was not Mozart's. We believe that it is a deliberately simple work, which Mozart composed following the cantata (K. 623); while not conferring on it any particular specificity, we consider it a continuation of the same spirit of brotherhood.

2

The Symbolism

Which of Mozart's works are to be recognized as Masonic seems set in stone by the List (see Appendix 1, p. 123). This grouping, simplistic and limiting, excludes a good number of works in which Masonic language or influence can be recognized or sensed if we look for the presence of symbols or references in them. Even though they may not have been written for the practice of rituals or ceremonies in the Lodge, they are nonetheless Masonic in their inspiration and architecture.

Nineteenth-century scholars, already little interested in Mozart's "officially" Masonic works, were even less disposed to investigations which might have revealed that other works, among some of his most important, were directly influenced by Masonic symbolism.

For about twenty years, as Roger Cotte has noted, a number of musicological studies tended, on the contrary, to conclude that Masonic spirituality occupies a place in Mozart's works that is equal to the importance of Lutheran Christianity in the inspiration of J. S. Bach.[1] If this judgment seems excessive, it at least has the merit of requiring us to look for Masonic inspiration in works not officially recognized as such. We are invited to conduct such research by none other than Alfred Einstein. "Mozart was a passionate and devoted freemason. . . . We have from Mozart not only a whole series of important works but in fact his entire production that is steeped in Masonic feeling; a good many of his works—and not only *The Magic Flute*—are Masonic even though the non-initiated may doubt that."[2] Jean and Brigitte Massin are also to be congratulated for their scrupulous research, which has brought to light the Masonic influence and its importance in a great number of Mozart's compositions.[3]

We intend to pursue the investigation that Einstein invites us to engage in: to analyze works that are incontestably Masonic, even though they are not recognized as such by the List, in order to determine why and in what respects they are Masonic.

Whatever insight they might have brought to their analysis of Mozart's works, Teodor de Wyzewa and Georges de Saint-Foix did not see this influence or turn their attention to it.[4]

Critical authors have widely varying approaches concerning Masonic influence and the presence of symbols in Mozart's work. In some cases, they are not freemasons, but have collected information from initiates in order to bolster their analysis. Their thought process often means well but they can neither understand nor translate what is essential, not having lived in an ongoing way the practice of ritual in a lodge. Their description is that of a landscape drawn from pictures, not from life.

In other cases, writers are freemasons whose research reflects actual knowledge of freemasonry, but when it comes to Mozart's works, they don't want to go as far as their privilege as initiates would permit. Their analysis remains honest but insufficient.

Yet others are freemasons, or say that they are, who take advantage of their membership in the Order to present an analysis that is deliberately complex, as if it were a question of a revelation bestowed on the reader. Their analysis seems to have been recast by their imaginations.

In reality, Mozart's Masonic symbolism is just as simple as the symbols on which it is based. The difficulty is to make its beauty understood and its profound meaning perceived.

How can references to Masonic symbolism be an authentic source of inspiration for Mozart? Musical analysis can allow us to see how he wove this symbolism into his writing so that his composition would lead, in its turn, toward a conferring of the sacred. This notion of conferring the sacred underlies all our consideration of Mozart as a freemason.

A Masonic assembly is characterized by its essential purpose, conferring of the sacred on the assembly through specificity of the liturgical act. Therefore, such conferring must at the same time characterize the music related to it. "We are no longer in the secular world," are the words the brothers in the Lodge repeat at the opening of every assembly. Conferring the sacred takes place solely through the community of spirit shared among brothers who are united at the same time and place, with the express intent of all those present to concentrate their spirit and their meditation on the content of the symbols. Conferring the sacred is not appropriate before the opening of the assembly and disappears upon its close. If, through the practice of a traditional ritual, an assembly presents a ceremonial character, that in itself is not a religious act and even less would the music accompanying it be religious.

Therefore, there is an opposition of processes between, on the one hand, a Masonic assembly that creates its own sense of the sacred and, on the other hand, a religious ceremony in which the liturgy is simply the outward expression of a pre-existent sacred process. This opposition also applies to the accompanying music.

Religious music is considered sacred because it is an integral part of a liturgy that is itself considered permanently sacred. This is why church music can be only illustrative when it accompanies the ceremony's unfolding (e.g., organ pieces are church music without being sacred in themselves). Otherwise, music takes on the quality of the sacred by osmosis from a text that is itself sacred, becoming in this way an integral part of the liturgy itself.

It is quite another case with music for which Masonic symbolism constitutes the very source of its inspiration, since the conferring of the sacred never exists before the performance. Indeed, the symbol is never sacred in itself; only through its evoking, under precise and rigorous conditions, can it lead to a conferring of the sacred. Thus, musical composition, since it transcribes the symbol, leads in itself to the sacred.

It is miraculous how Mozart understood the esthetic and spiritual potential of this transcription, realizing perfectly the appropriateness between the message contained in the symbol and the inspiration carried by the music. The spirit of the listener, whoever he may be, rises above the secular world. By having intensely lived this ritual and the practice of universal symbols, Mozart was completely aware of what such music would bring to his brothers and, moreover, to all people in all times.

At the opening of the work of the Lodge—an opening (as we have said) made possible only through a ritual that permits the conveyance of the sacred to that place and that occasion—the Master declares, in essence, "We are no longer in the secular world . . . let us raise our hearts in brotherhood and direct our gaze toward the light." We need to keep returning to this invocation, which must be an integral part of every work that Mozart crafted with Masonic inspiration. It is appropriate to keep it in mind when we intend to analyze a work that seems Masonic. This invocation also makes it possible to understand the motivation and logic according to which Mozart wrote the score. It remains the criterion for reference that allows us to set aside works that we might be tempted to consider Masonic, or, on the contrary, to help us recognize as Masonic works that we might have dismissed in a superficial examination.

Mozart understood the essential quality and significance of this invocation because he experienced it at the opening of each assembly. His deep belief in the Masonic ideal revealed to him that reaching the light, beauty, and a world above the secular one became possible by living through the symbols. This belief apparently became for Wolfgang a comfort and ideal whose expression is reflected in his inspiration.

Works on the List (except for the operas) were all written for explicitly Masonic purposes. The uninitiated can easily recognize them as such because they accompany a text that openly glorifies Masonic thought. In this case, we are dealing with hymns, songs, or cantatas without reference to symbols and therefore without conveying the sacred. Other works from the List are those that illustrate, through music, a moment in the ceremony or one of the components of the ritual (generally a slow march). In this case, he does not use voices; only wind instruments take part, forming what, in Lodges, are still called "columns of harmony." It could be pointed out that such instruments are precisely, by their nature, linked to breath, which itself is a symbol of life. Two adagios, one for two basset-horns and bassoon (K. 410) and a second for two clarinets and three basset-horns (K. 411), are perfect examples of this.

To understand Masonic influence in the works of Mozart that have been colored in this way, we must move beyond the List. The classification must be based on a different criterion. Works are of a Masonic character when they belong to rituals or refer to Masonic thought. In this case we are speaking of works for rituals or special occasions. However, a work is truly Masonic when it is inspired by symbols and their content. We will see that, in this case, a musical composition adopts the symbol and immediately abandons it; however, it retains from the symbol the creative meaning of a cloaking within the sacred. From that point on, the whole work reflects the movement toward another world.

The term "inspiration" as used in this book requires some explanation. When we say that a work is not inspired, we simply mean that Masonic symbolism does not make up the real creative impulse for it.

Beginning with this distinction, we can launch our study according to the following classification, which we will use as we proceed:

Works of a Masonic Character
Ritual, or for an Occasion

- Works that are officially recognized as such and are on the List, such as the cantatas and the Adagio (K. 411)
- Works that are not on the List but are of a Masonic character, such as the slow movements of the Divertimenti (K. 439b) or the Adagio for Basset Horn (K. 580a)

Not ritual, but may be on the List

- Works that have the advantage of bringing to our ears a characteristic musical language and a writing style specifically imbued with the intentional majesty of the ritual, occasionally embellished by the unrestrained citation of meaningful symbols, such as the song "O heiliges Band" and the drama *Thamos*. If a symbol appears, it is only to justify the Masonic character of the piece. Mozart musically cites certain symbols—among them the most characteristic and understandable for the non-initiate, such as the number three and the beats. But in this, the reference to symbols stops with only the exterior envelope being presented.

Works of Masonic inspiration

- Works that are inspired by the value of the symbol's content and its power of evocation, which is at the heart of musical creation. We will concentrate on these works specifically as we proceed.

3

From Symbols to Music

In the ritual and solely by its practice, the freemason is accorded the possibility of leaving the "secular world" in order to "raise his heart in brotherhood and turn his gaze toward the light." The investigation and analysis of Masonic influence in Mozart's works has meaning only in reference to this invocation and the living of it.

To live this invocation and the ritual to which it belongs as Wolfgang lived them is the only way we can understand the sources of his inspiration and follow the progression of his musical works—compositions which are equally capable of leading us from the profane to the sacred. Like ritual, the music speaks of rigor, strength, beauty, serenity, and light. Mozart knew that the musical transcription of the symbol he invoked made it possible to reach such a vision. This transcription of symbols, however, is not a process such as that with illustrative music, which proceeds by citations supporting the process of "doing freemasonry." The uninitiated listener does not need to know or recognize the symbols or appreciate their value in a work that they have inspired; he need only experience, by means of this music, an approach to another world. On the other hand, the initiate who listens to the work gains the opportunity to relive the emotion and feelings that he experiences during the ceremony among his brothers.

As soon as he enters the Lodge, the freemason is surrounded by the most meaningful visual symbols. They are always there before him: the floor layout itself (the black and white checkerboard tiling); the three steps that lead to the Grand Master's chair; the lights placed on the three columns representing the three orders of Doric, Ionian, and Corinthian; the two columns symbolizing those of the Temple of Solomon, the sun and the moon, and so on. At certain moments in the ceremony, the freemason will hear auditory symbols: the beating of a mallet or the clapping of hands. By capturing these same symbols in the musical composition and transposing their content into harmonies, Mozart built his Masonic compositions.

Other musicians as well as Mozart used this kind of composition: Haydn in "The Creation" (when God creates light), in three of his Parisian symphonies (Nos. 84, 85, and 86), and in his Symphony No. 98 in B flat major (apparently written in Mozart's memory); Christoph Willibald Gluck in his opera *Orpheus*, through the symbolism reflected throughout; E. T. A. Hoffmann in his first symphony in E flat major (considered the "Masonic key"), also written in homage to Mozart; Beethoven in the adagio of his Quartet No. 7 in F major, opus 59/1, when he dedicates the second movement to a dead brother with an acacia on his grave (a symbol characteristic of the third degree). We should also mention several French freemason composers who used Masonic elements, such as François Giroult in "le Déluge" and François Devienne in the slow movements of some of his trios for flute.

Without specifying a hierarchical order among them, the symbols Mozart uses in order to "edify" the composition so that it will reflect his ideal are essentially the following:

The threefold element, which appears in his composition in several forms

- The key with three sharps or three flats, the major or minor third being a symbol of ideal harmony, dotted rhythm being a symbol of time
- The march, always slow and of a processional character
- Space, based on the visual elements of the Lodge and practices in the ritual
- The transition from the unbuilt or unformed to rigor, "from raw stone to the cube of stone," from chaos to order
- Beats (or beating: the "knocks" of Masonic ritual)
- The steps that lead up to the Orient

We would be opening not only a debate but a controversy to suggest that such symbols could be a real source of inspiration and we would be then ascribing the power of musical creation to these symbols.

Let us take the characteristic example of the use of three "points" or "signature marks" in the musical key, which has given rise to a great number of polemics. It is true that in works for special occasions just as in inspirational works, Mozart often uses the key of E flat major (or its related key C minor), which carries three "points" in the key. Is this the reason that E flat major is the Masonic key more than any other one?

Remy Stricker disagrees with Jacques Chailley and Jean and Brigitte Massin, who in fact consider E flat major to be the principal Masonic key.[1] He states, "Let us not conclude that all Mozart's works in E flat major are related to freemasonry. In fact, what are the keys used by Mozart in music he composed for Masonic ceremonies? Only two cantatas are in E flat (K. 429 and K. 471); the other works (K. 619, 623, 483, 484 and 468) are in different keys." He concludes that these musicologists are mistaken and that their analysis "leads to a dead end." In fact, it is Stricker's analysis that is wrong. His study, as he himself stresses, is based solely on the works made for ceremonies—that is, related to functions—and he does not realize that by doing so he diminishes interest in those works. We know that in the case of these works, the Masonic message is expressed overtly and explicitly, without any need to call upon a symbol to carry it—such as using a key in three flats. It should be noted that Stricker, as if by presentiment, intentionally excludes from his analysis the Funeral Ode in C minor (K. 477). This work is not "overt." It follows musically the theme of the death of Hiram and the rebirth (ceremony of the third degree, that of the Master mason). The threefold symbol of C minor and that of the processional march are at the basis of the inspiration for this ode.

It would be a mistake to systematically look for a symbolic influence in any of Mozart's works written with three flats. But it would be equally mistaken to fail—or refuse—to recognize a Masonic influence in works written with these three signs on the pretext that they don't appear on the List.

THE NUMBER THREE

Like all approaches to the sacred since the world's origin, freemasonry has considered the number three a sacred number: a symbol of perfection or divinity. It appears in the text of rituals and in the course of carrying out ceremonies. In the Lodge it is never far from each brother and continually invites him to ponder the deep universal message that it has always carried. Mozart was not at all obsessed with the alchemy of numbers, but he was convinced enough of the creative power of the threefold symbol to use it freely where necessary to express his thought or inspiration. As a harmonic or rhythmic element, it may appear in various forms.

The three "points"

We have seen that the number three, represented by three points in the key signature at the beginning of the score, determines the key. Researchers, while recognizing the importance of the threefold element, seem not to take it into account except in the case of three flats; in that case, only works in E flat major or its related key C minor would be of Masonic inspiration. This cannot be justified on either musical or Masonic grounds. Besides, it is sadly restrictive. If the symbolic value is determined solely by the presence of three points, then three sharps ought to imply an identical

Examples of sharps and flats

symbolic value. From the point of view of freemasonry, there is nothing to contradict this assertion.

If we did not take sharps into consideration we would omit two of Mozart's admirable and fundamentally Masonic works: the Quartet in A major (K. 464), written in January 1785, the day after his initiation; and the Concerto for Clarinet (K. 622), written for his brother Anton Stadler three months before Mozart's death. It is clear that keys with flats seemed to have been considered, without any serious justification, as more symbolic than keys with sharps.

Having three flats in the key ought to catch our attention, but their presence or absence is not a determining factor in the symbolic inspiration of the work. Chailley speaks of having been aware of an effect that was more restful, profound, and moving when the Chorale of César Franck's Sixth Beatitude was transposed from F sharp to E flat.[2] The simultaneity of the three signature points and the atmosphere of the key in flats, which is more touching in its harmony, have conferred on the E flat key a supremacy that is, however, not justified from the Masonic point of view. This is why the Concerto for Piano No. 9 (K. 271), although in E flat major, is not of Masonic inspiration, while Concerto No. 20 in D minor (K. 466), although having only a single flat, is indeed of such inspiration since it invokes other symbols that are convincing and just as creative as the symbol of three signature points.

Let us consider the case when three points no longer appear in the key. Contrary to what some authors try to show, these different keys are not symbolic, except for one, the key of C major, the pure key, since it requires no signature point in the key—in fact, such a point would be a blemish. This is why it is difficult to accept the thinking of authors who strive to justify a symbolism in the other keys. Philippe Autexier writes that the key of D major (with two

sharps) carries a symbolic meaning since in German it is called D,*
corresponding to the Greek letter delta, whose triangular shape we
know to be important in freemasonry.[3] This approach is meaning-
less in traditional symbolism and is even more devoid of meaning
in universal symbolism. The reference to a limiting specificity, such
as the alphabet of a European language, can have no real value. In
addition, using an analysis of the same kind, this author likewise
sees in a composition in G major [*sol majeur* in French] a work
imbued with light since in Italian, "sol" means sun. It is clear that
we cannot reduce a symbolism whose nature is precisely its uni-
versality to such specifics—still less can we ascribe to these details
the power of inspiration.

Masonic symbolism has no reason to recognize the distinction,
according to which we would rise in the hierarchy of Masonic
degrees, because the work which is intended to illustrate the rise
would assign an additional flat each time. According to Autexier,
the number of flats expresses the degree of the freemason.[4] The
Adagio (K. 410) in F major (with one flat) would be destined for
the Entered Apprentice, the first degree; the song "Fellowcraft's
Journey" (K. 468), the second degree, requires the key of B flat
(two flats); finally, the cantata "Die Maurerfreude" (K. 471), dedicated to a Master mason, i.e., the third degree, requires three flats.
In fact, since only the threefold element implies a symbolic value,
it is hard to understand how these critics manage to recognize as
Masonic those works that depend on an increasing number of flats
leading up to the number three.

---

*[The keys are named in French with their names in the scale used for singing (do, re,
mi, fa, sol, la, ti, do), so here the key being spoken of is "re." Both English and German use the letters A to G as names for the keys (with "do" being equal to "C" and
so on). — *Trans.*]

We find this same procedure, but in reverse, in Jacques Chailley's analysis of *The Magic Flute*. He says: "Let us consider the paradigm of one side and then the other side of the center point of C major; C major itself is without either sharp or flat (God speaks in C major, says Gounod). Then we have on one side the keys with flats and on the other the keys with sharps. The first side represents wisdom and the second mundane light-heartedness. From the mixture of this symbolism with that of the number three proceeds the hieratic preeminence of E flat major."[5] Chailley is right in insisting on the preeminence of this key, but his argument in justifying it has no connection to any viable Masonic data. E flat has a preeminence because it contains the symbolic number three, not because it has flats. There cannot be a mixture between two symbolisms for the simple reason that a flat has never been a symbol in itself. Like Autexier, Chailley analyzes what he means by adapting the symbol to the needs of his argument. "The framework of E flat is amputated and reduced to two flats for the aria (B flat) of the Queen of the Night, and in the end reduced to a single flat (F natural) for the combat of the Queen with the Initiates." We could jokingly say that it's a good thing that the choice of keys stopped there, otherwise the successive amputation of flats would have led, from one diminution to the next, until there were none at all and we arrive at C major which is, however, the key of God—and that would be illogical. These analyses, conscientious and well meaning though they may be, do not take into consideration the reality of Masonic ritual alone. It is inconceivable that a symbol can weaken or become stronger. It is what it is, forever unalterable, and has been so since the beginning of time.

It is not in the Lodge that Mozart would have followed such a teaching in Masonic musicography because symbolism is not imposed using technical rules of harmony. He simply knew, through his experience, that the number three was fundamental and carried a message. In the Lodge, this number underlies the three luminaries of freemasonry (the Compass, the T-Square, and the Book of Sacred Law). He would keep this number in mind and quite naturally knew how to have recourse to it when he was composing a work whose inspiration referred to it.

Intervals of thirds

The superimposition of thirds, major or minor, constitutes a perfect chord and creates a serene harmony that has been recognized as such since Pythagoras first analyzed it. Thirds can be expressed either in the form of a non-arpeggiated chord (in which all the notes are played simultaneously) or as an arpeggiated chord (where the notes are played in succession). Thirds can also result from the superimposition, at this interval, of several melodic lines.

E. T. A. Hoffmann describes his vision of thirds in "Ritter Glück" ("The Knight Glück"), a short story in his *Musikalisch Novellen*. "It is the supreme moment, contact with the Eternal, the ineffable; behold the sun: it's the perfect chord (*Dreiklang*) in

Examples of the superimposition of thirds
Above: Non-arpeggiated chords
Below: Arpeggiated chords

which three notes like stars melt over you, enveloping you in their fingers of flame." He goes on: "Two colossal structures, decked with shining appendages, are moving toward me: the Tonic and the Fifth. They carry me away but the Eye smiles and says to me, 'I know that your soul is pierced by an ardent desire. That sweet and tender adolescent, the Third will come between these giants. You will hear his sweet voice.'" We can see from reading this quotation, as overdrawn as it may be, what vision an initiate might experience from a simple interval of three notes and what an interpretation he might ascribe to it. Given the description of this vision that personifies the third and intentionally brings in the symbol of the eye, we cannot doubt Hoffmann's deep understanding in a work inspired by freemasonry.

Mozart, a freemason like Hoffmann, knows that the third, either in the form of a chord or in intervals expressed in a melodic line, is a symbol bearing harmony. Its use is not necessarily an indication of symbolism; it may be for the composer simply an expression of serenity. But conversely, when Mozart wants to express more particularly the serenity of Masonic thought, he turns to the interval of the third because he knows its evocative power. We need to cite in this regard, given their importance, the theme stated in thirds of the first movement of Symphony No. 39 in E flat major (K. 543) and the themes of the first and second movements of the Divertimento in E flat major, the "Puchberg Trio" (K. 563), which use this same mode of harmonic expression.

Presence of three kinds of instruments
The presence of three kinds of instruments does not constitute a source of symbolic inspiration. Its Masonic meaning would be only factual. Certain musicologists have attached an unjustified

meaning to it. The Quartets in A major (K. 464) and C major (K. 465), composed by Mozart a few weeks after his initiation, as well as the Quintet in D major (K. 593), are just as much bearers of Masonic thought as the "Puchberg" Trio. If Masonic compositions have three kinds of instruments, it is because, in the eighteenth century, works performed in the Lodges were generally for three kinds of wind instruments (bassoon, oboe, basset horn). Besides, these compositions were performed to accompany special occasions.

Ternary rhythm

The number three is a symbol that can be expressed equally well using rhythm. It is essentially a pointed rhythm (♩. ♪). The ternary element appears twice: The dotted note corresponds to three times the value of the dot and the rhythmic theme has no meaning unless it uses the cell of three notes. It is clear that if we were to walk to this rhythm we would limp. Limping has a deep symbolic meaning: Oedipus limped and the layman, precisely to recall this myth, limps when entering the Lodge to be initiated.

The dotted rhythm brings to the musical line a slightly breathless, panting quality, appropriate to the difficulty of making one's way toward the light. The efforts called for are thus transcribed musically. This impression is particularly vivid in the introductory adagio of Symphony No. 39. We shall see, regarding the symphony itself, how this "portico," a real Propylaea, leads toward the light.* Mozart's intention was that, among the symbols supporting this portico, the ternary rhythm from the dotted note forms one element in his architecture.

---

*[Propylaea is the name of the entranceway to the Acropolis in Athens. —*Trans.*]

Steps Toward the Altar

Moving up steps to approach the altar or the temple has always been a universal symbol. It is among the easiest to recognize in a musical score. In the Lodge, in order to reach the Orient where the Grand Master is seated, you have to mount three steps. Moreover, these steps, designed as part of the ritual tableau at the center of the Masonic hall, are always visible to the freemason. In musical terms, they take the shape of ascending triplets at the beginning of the work. The listener easily perceives this especially descriptive form of imagery. The musical form appears to the ear just as the steps appear to the eye: the mark of a shift in levels.

In the essay in which he draws a parallel between Mozart and the poet Friedrich Hölderin, Michel Tamisier speaks of this device as "the menacing thrust used to begin the Concerto in D minor, the 'Prague' Symphony, and the 'Jupiter' Symphony."[6] He sees in this thrust the expression of an ascendant theme that is characteristic of Mozart's genius. In addition, he is quite right in grouping these three

Concerto in D minor (K. 466)

Symphony in C major (K. 551)

33

compositions and noticing that all three use a similar musical device, the ascending thrust, so evocative for him, although he is unaware that this device is the transcription of the symbol of the steps leading to the Orient. In perceiving accurately—but unconsciously—the symbol of the rising steps, Tamisier brings together those works in which he sees the same inspiration.

SPACE

Symbols of time and space are constituent parts of the ritual. They represent the world in its present state and its unfolding. The initiation and other ceremonies of the Lodge continually draw on these symbols. The symbol of time cannot give rise to a specific musical transcription since it is immaterial and in that respect identical to the music itself. In these two cases, we have signs that cannot be cast into form.

With regard to space, at least two essential symbols are always before the freemason's eyes. The first is that defined by the Orient and the Occident. From the beginning of the world, it has been experienced through the movement of the sun in the sky. Recall how the Greeks represented it: in the pediments in the Parthenon that portray the birth of Athena. Moreover, this space is "drawn" by the two rows into which the brothers are divided on either side of the Grand Master's chair, which is located at the Orient. Two brothers, the Wardens, stand for these two rows through a particular function.* They represent all their brothers and speak in their name. Their responses, which alternate with the questions posed

---

*[In Masonic references, the French term "Surveillant," meaning one who watches or witnesses, is sometimes used instead of Warden. — *Trans.*]

by the Grand Master, seem to formulate orally the limits of the space, especially at the opening and closing of the proceedings.

The second form of the symbol of space is that of the alternating black and white squares, which form the Mosaic Flooring positioned at the center of the Lodge. The music transcribes their alternation using a similar form of musical "responses."

Space is easy to symbolize in sound. Musical phrases, even short ones, seem to respond to one another. Mozart treats this technique of the alternation and "response" of sounds with a remarkable mastery. As the breadth of these musical responses surges, the space they define then seems to billow, a growth in extent that often is tied closely with the symbol of ascent. These two symbols lead the listener to a summit where his gaze extends toward infinity and his thought toward hope. Anyone can be led to such a summit, but only the initiate knows how to recognize the nature of the work's inspiration and share the thinking behind the vision Mozart offers.

The theme of the *andante con motto* of Symphony No. 39 is expressed in this way by alternating responses. Not only do two short phrases converse with each other, but each of them is expressed by different instruments—strings on one side and wind instruments on the other. In this way, Mozart places the listener in the center of a space whose boundaries are defined by sound.

FROM THE UNFORMED TO RIGOR, FROM DARKNESS TO LIGHT

The transition from the unformed to rigor, from the unbuilt to the constructed, from raw stone to the cube of stone, and from darkness to the light, following the actual terms of the ritual, is a very strong Masonic symbol because it characterizes initiation.

Symphony No. 39 in E flat major (K. 543)

This symbol, easy to transcribe musically and a bearer of great meaning, is (along with the number three) one of those most often used by Mozart. Once heard, it is easily recognizable and can be grasped by a layman. This usage is also found in the works of the freemason composers cited previously. The transcription of this symbol precedes and always introduces the theme of the first movement of the work. When the theme of this first movement is simple and rigorous, then, proportionally, the writing of this veritable "portico" will be complex and intentionally chaotic. This deliberate opposition between two kinds of writing expresses the symbol. Its spelling out will require a certain time, across several measures, comparable to that needed for the construction of a temple or the attainment of light. Mozart resorts to this form of writing in the second work that he composed after his initiation, the Quartet in C major (K. 465), known precisely for this reason as "Dissonance." The opening musical theme—in which Mozart's contemporaries saw an accumulation of wrong notes that they would have liked to correct—in fact extends slowly over twenty-two bars until the moment when there is launched, in C major, the simple and luminous melody of the theme of the first movement, which is necessarily characterized by the rigor and perfection of its construction. The same transcription of this symbol opens Symphony No. 38 in D major, "Prague" (K. 504), and Symphony No. 39 in E flat major (K. 543); both are examples of symbolic influence.

The use of these symbols was not a constraint for Mozart. It is clear that a work that claims Masonic inspiration must, to express that morality, depend on symbolism; it cannot express such an idea or vision in any way other than by reference to the content of the ritual. The great difference between Mozart and other composers resides in the fact that Mozart, a confirmed initiate, never considered the use of a symbol to be a restricting obligation. On the contrary, by transcribing it, he gave free rein to a power of creativity identical to that which he experienced through the practice and living of the ritual.

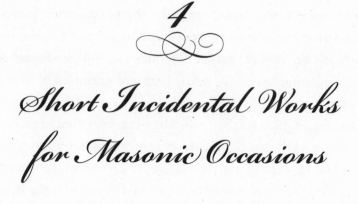

4

Short Incidental Works
for Masonic Occasions

Mozart, now an initiate, was able to write indisputably Masonic music without, however, the actual symbols of freemasonry being a source of inspiration. In this category are works that we have termed "for special occasions" but which express very directly the initiate's vision of the Royal Art and his knowledge of the ritual. Such works are not on the List.

The research of Jean and Brigitte Massin brought attention to these numerous compositions created during the course of three years following Mozart's initiation.

Most of these compositions are short. They were written for musician friends in a warm and fraternal setting. In the Lodge, they were likely performed by brothers with whom Mozart, outside the assemblies, had ongoing relationships in everyday life. These works, initially intended for Masonic occasions and illustrative of ritual sequences, were probably used later as movements integrated into works that were not Masonic. This is all the more likely since they were written for instruments that form columns of harmony (mentioned above). In this way, they could very naturally be included in divertimenti or serenades for wind instruments. Musicians performing them would know how to identify in these treasures the parts that came from the friend and those that also came from the brother.

Five Divertimenti (K. 439b)

It is almost certain that a Masonic character applies to the slow movements of the Divertimenti for two clarinets (or basset horns) and bassoon (K. 439b). Certain melodic lines appear to be sketches of what would later become great works. The compositions are not dated because Mozart did not record them in the catalogue he kept of his own works. In the Köchel catalog they are included only at the end of the *notturni* (K. 436, 437, 438, and 439), the latter dated 1783. There is a dating error here. Wyzewa and Saint-Foix quite rightly group these compositions with K. 487, which is dated July 27, 1786. In fact it is more logical to group these Divertimenti with works that share a similar character and inspiration, and to pinpoint their composition within a fairly brief period around July 1786. In addition, we should note that on August 5, 1786, Mozart composed one of his most poetic works, commonly called the "Billiards" Trio for piano, clarinet, and viola (K. 498), dedicated to his freemason friends, the Jacquin family. This trio can then logically be considered a conclusion to this bouquet of works. We can be assured that, during a period of one or two months before August 1786, Mozart composed a group of works that had an intimate and undeniably Masonic character. Not written for performance before large audiences, they were intended as gifts, to remain among friends and especially brothers.

The slow movements of these Divertimenti are quite comparable to the Adagio for two clarinets and three basset horns (K. 411). There is no doubt that this adagio is of a Masonic character. In this regard, Roger Cotte shows how the writing seems to coincide with the practice of the ritual.[1] Its slow second melodic line supports the march of the brothers as they proceed toward the opening or the closing of the Lodge; this melody is interrupted by silences that correspond precisely to the interruptions in the procession necessitated by the practice of ritual gestures in the ceremony. The slow movements of the Divertimenti proceed following a rhythm identical to that of the Adagio (K. 411), but what is essential above all for understanding their Masonic character is that they have the same interruptions. It would be appropriate today to recognize the *andantes* of the Five Divertimenti as also being Masonic. At the present time, certain Lodges have, in a way, "unearthed" them in order to include them in carrying out their ceremonies— something Mozart would certainly have wished.

Adagio in C major (K. 580a)

It makes sense in this section to include the Adagio in C major for English horn accompanied by two basset horns (K. 580a). It is from the same period (1789) as the Quintet for clarinet in A major, called the "Stadler" Quintet (K. 581), and as another sketch for a Quintet in F major, also for clarinet and wind instruments (K. 580b), of which only fragments remain. The creation of several works during the same short period for characteristically Masonic instruments deserves special attention when one of them in particular is offered to a brother, as is the case with the "Stadler." We are justified in thinking that this adagio—written for this kind of wind instrument, using a characteristically processional rhythm, and apparently dedicated to his brothers (considering the date of composition)—is undoubtedly also a Masonic work. Mozart must have attached a certain importance to it, having given it great beauty and a very pure musical theme. This beauty, combined with the profundity of the inspiration, makes this song truly "religious." The serenity that arises from it is exactly the same as what we see in both ritual Masonic works and certain passages of the masses he wrote in his youth. This is the case to such an extent that the melodic theme of this adagio is the same one that Mozart chose in his composition of the *Ave Verum* the year he died. This hymn, written on the occasion of the feast of Corpus Christi for his friend Anton Stoll, is actually a Masonic "hymn" composed for another purpose, but in the same spirit, a few years before. There is nothing surprising about this. For Wolfgang, Masonic faith and religious faith became one at the end of his life. Using the same song, he celebrated both one faith and the other, making clear in doing so the equal value he attributed to each. In his last year, there was no longer any difference in belief, nor consequently in inspiration, between the Masonic theme of the Adagio in C major and this Christian hymn, just as there is no difference between the Funeral Ode and the Requiem Mass.

5

❦

Works of a Masonic Character That Are Not Ritualistic

These works are very limited in number and easy to recognize as Masonic but were composed by Mozart before his initiation. His freemason friends commissioned them while he was still an adolescent. They indicate the close ties between his family and freemasons, ties that would later play a decisive role in Mozart's becoming a member of freemasonry himself.

According to our research, these works are of very different scope. There are two short *lieder* (songs) and the theatrical music for a German-language drama, *Thamos, König in Ägypten (Thamos, King of Egypt)*. Neither was intended for a ritual or a special occasion during assemblies in a Lodge. Moreover, since he was not yet initiated, Mozart could only use a clearly explicit text with them, and symbolism in them could appear only in an illustrative way.

Two songs come into this category: "An die Freude" ("To Joy") (K. 53) and "O heiliges Band der Freundschaft" ("O Hallowed Bond of Friendship") (K. 148). We know the history of the first of these. It is composed of couplets, having a very simple melodic line, and is accompanied by a single keyboard. Mozart composed this song at age twelve for Dr. Joseph Wolff of Olmültz. What did he experience? Was he marked by these first contacts? With its simple words, the text he was given certainly did not put him off since he was very willing to set it to music. The song "O heiliges Band" presents a problem in dating. In the Köchel catalog the date of its composition is 1772. However, according to the format and the texture of the paper used, Wysewa and Saint-Foix date it at the end of 1784.[1] The text, from a collection of Masonic songs, makes the composition totally "overt." Mozart limits himself to musical accompaniment, but one of deep seriousness. Because of its attractiveness, this song could easily have been used in the ceremonies of an assembly, being as it is a real Masonic hymn imbued with dignity. The care that Mozart brought to such a modest work makes us think that he wrote it knowing how it would actually be used. This assumes that he had freely and openly discussed it with his friends who were to become (or already were) his brothers, especially if, as we now believe, its composition was from late 1784 or early 1785. This interpretation, justified by the tenor of the music, would suggest a composition date situated in the vicinity of the time of his initiation, thereby confirming the opinion of Wyzewa and Saint-Foix.

THAMOS (K. 345)

It is fitting to restore to this opera the importance that Mozart himself attached to it. Writing from Vienna on February 15, 1783, he thanked his father for forwarding him the score for *Thamos,* which had been left behind in Salzburg. "I am really annoyed," he said, "not to be able to use the music that I wrote for *Thamos.* Not having been a success, this play has become a discredited work. It should be put on again just for the music. It's really a pity."

The libretto is solely of Masonic inspiration. Mozart worked on it on two occasions, in 1773 and again in 1779. While in Vienna in 1773, he received from Baron von Gebler the commission to compose music for the latter's play *Thamos,* a heroic German drama. Gebler, an influential freemason, who would later play a decisive role in Mozart's joining the Order, was Vice-Chancellor of Vienna. After conferring with other freemasons, including the composer Gluck, Gebler entrusted the work to Wolfgang, who at the time was only seventeen. The friendly early relations with Dr. Wolff were not so distant, and yet what a road he had traveled in between! Mozart and his father maintained regular contact with freemasons, and Wolfgang certainly became aware, during these few short years, of the spirit of the Masonic order, so close to the *Aufklärung* that was also a formative element in his thinking. He grew to know its fraternal character and this attracted him more strongly every day. *Thamos* provided Mozart with the opportunity to express the feelings that the text inspired in him. He was not limited to simple musical accompaniment. In fact, Leopold reported, "this new composition calls on all of Wolfgang's forces." We need to recognize in *Thamos* the respectful opinion that Mozart experienced in being exposed to freemasonry and its philosophy, since the indisputable depth of the music shows clearly the interest that he displayed in the play's moral philosophy.

The work begins with a chorale in C major whose grandeur is comparable to what characterizes the greatest of his future compositions, especially *The Magic Flute*—of which *Thamos* seems to be the unintended precursor. The spirit of the play is profoundly religious. The music could have been composed for a Mass; indeed, it is closer to the Mass in C minor than those written to satisfy the requests of Archbishop Colleredo. The orchestration and the part played by the chorales are of an exceptional richness. We find here, like a seed, the style and the writing that will later be picked up again in the works where he expresses the apotheosis.

The second part is an interlude, also in C minor; its beginning warrants special attention. Indeed, the first measures are made up of six beats (or six chords), but set out three times in groups of two. It is tempting to read something into this example, but it would be a mistake. Mozart would have certainly learned by hearsay that three "knocks" are a feature of Masonic ritual. Also, after having so magnificently translated a religious vision of the subject in the first chorale, he wanted to convey the Masonic character of *Thamos* by means of "branding." Knowingly, Mozart struck three times, but used two "knocks," a perfect example of narrative rather than ritualistic character. To be ritualistic, he would have needed three single strikes or three strikes three times. This same "error" in the beats, using the famous five blows, was later to mark the first measures of the *The Magic Flute* overture (but deliberate by then, since Mozart had learned in the meantime to understand the exact meaning of this drumming in the Lodge). It is not only through the beats (the knocking theme) that we can approach these works. We can approach them equally well through the structure of the theme that follows the first measures. These two works are identical in their conception and their writing. This theme, in which the musical line seems to run on as if crazed, may have represented in Mozart's mind the wandering that troubles someone who has not found wisdom.

From 1773 on, Mozart's interest in freemasonry was clearly becoming a serious intellectual concern. His striving to understand it and translate its spirit and ethic may have allowed him, starting at that time, to conceive of this new moral philosophy as a substitute or complement to his beliefs, which at the time were shaken by the life imposed on him by Salzburg society and his employer, the Archbishop. We glimpse in these works from adolescence, which absorbed him so intensely and to which he devoted such care, the starting point of a thought process that was clearly to culminate at the end of his life in the creation of *The Magic Flute*.

Mozart's first return to *Thamos* was in 1779. Collaborating with Johann Boehm, a violinist and director of an important theatre troupe visiting Salzburg, he decided to return to Gebler's Masonic drama, which had been completely unsuccessful in its original version. Mozart substituted a melodrama for the interlude (No. 3) in the initial composition, but more importantly, he added a new final sequence (No. 7) composed of a solo by the Grand Priest followed by a final chorale. In this reworking of the drama, Mozart displayed a remarkable light-handedness in the orchestration. The force of supplementary sequence No. 7 confers an astonishing breadth to the work as a whole.

As of 1779, Mozart has not yet acquired a knowledge of the entire range of values of the symbols or of their hieratic content, but the musical expression of the drama nevertheless makes clear that he was very familiar with what Masonic thought represented.

Thamos was a foreshadowing of future great works and already contained the essence of what was to endow them with greatness. In this regard, we find in *The Magic Flute* the beats from the overture of *Thamos* and, in the scene of the damnation of Don Juan, the thrust and dramatic tension that characterize the Grand Priest's solo. The use of the same D minor key would also help justify, if any further justification were necessary, the close relationship between these two works. Finally, the Grand Priest in *Thamos* expresses, with the same power of conviction, what Sarastro would later express in *The Magic Flute*. The inspiration and writing are of the same character and the bass voices are identical.

Thamos is therefore an "overtly" Masonic work because it was composed following a Masonic text that, six years later, was completed with a solo and a chorale that made it even more Masonic. This drama is not a work in which symbol is a fundamental element inspiring the composition; the written text carries the message. Nevertheless, we can say that it is illuminated by a deep Masonic faith. This proves two things: that Mozart was already very well acquainted with Masonic knowledge, although not yet with its ritual and practice; and that despite that lack, he already foresaw clearly what initiation would bring him and how it would strengthen him and allow him to live by an ethic that already seemed like a new faith.

Mozart would return to *Thamos* a number of times; its success was less important to him than the work and hope it represented. It was completed in 1779, but Mozart did more. He added to it his Symphony No. 26 in E flat major (K. 184), which he had written in 1773, as an overture. By doing this, he hoped to give the drama a more solid and broad structure and make it more adaptable to being staged.

Perhaps as a mark of affection for his *Thamos,* Mozart later reused three chorales from it (Scenes 1, 6, and 7a) as musical accompaniment to two church hymns and a German canticle. The Massins concluded quite rightly that judging by the correspondence, the music was reworked for a third time, adapted to the libretto of the opera *Lanassa* in 1783. As far as an original work is concerned, *Lanassa,* not *Thamos,* garnered success. Mozart even had the opportunity to hear it in Frankfurt in 1790 in a somewhat distorted form. The texts of the libretti were not the same, but the music spoke again to Mozart of what his hopes for it had been.

What can we say about Symphony No. 26, wrongly called the "Lanassa" Symphony today? We should recall that Mozart had already made it the overture for *Thamos.* Later, after the combined opera-symphony became *Lanassa,* the symphony acquired the name of the opera. The symphony dates from the spring of 1773 and is therefore a few months earlier than *Thamos.* If Mozart, not yet having undergone his initiation, was only able to use Masonic symbols in an illustrative way for the opera, it is all the more the case for the older work, the symphony. In 1779, Mozart chose this symphony as an addition to the opera. By that time, he had several other symphonies from which to choose. Or did he? The elevation of thought in *Thamos* called for an overture of the same order, and he knew that Symphony No. 26 in E flat major was Masonic, as was *Thamos* itself. Its second movement consists of a slow majestic procession whose meaning we now understand. For Mozart the work was clearly Masonic, which is why he naturally used it as the overture to Gebler's drama.

In addition, we should point out the similarity in keys. *Thamos* is in C minor and the symphony is in E flat major: two related keys that require three "points" in the key signature. It seems then that

Mozart, under friendly influences, was trying out the creation of a large-scale Masonic work without yet knowing precisely the hieratic value of the symbols, but which his genius has allowed him to intuit. The vision that he had always had of beauty meant that his view of the world was different from that of others. In December 1784, freemasonry initiated a man whose genius had already revealed to him the light.

THE FUNERAL ODE (K. 477)

This work, so exceptional in its inspiration and its musical language, can be considered a turning point between compositions for ritual and those inspired by symbolism.

Wyzewa and Saint-Foix judge this work to be "one of the most elevated pieces in all of music and especially revealing of the greatness of the soul of the composer." Einstein writes of it "as one of the most magnificent of Mozart's pieces, like a religious composition forming a link between the Mass in C minor (K. 427) of 1781 and the Requiem."[2] Before any commentary here, Einstein's judgment deserves close attention because it totally confirms our analysis and interpretation of the import of its Masonic inspiration. Is it not astonishing that through this work, one declared Masonic by Mozart himself, Einstein recognizes a link between the two greatest Catholic and religious works from the pen of the Master of Salzburg?

It has now been proven that Mozart did not compose the Funeral Ode on the occasion of the funerals of two of his brothers in freemasonry: Georg August von Mecklenburg, who died November 6, 1785, and Franz Esterhazy, who died the next day. Mozart composed it in July 1785, eight months after his initiation, but did not enter it into his catalogue until November, upon the death of these two brothers. The Funeral Ode was performed for a ceremony organized in their memory, but not for their funerals. It is still performed today by freemasons in their funeral ceremonies.

What was the real reason Mozart composed this work in July? It is Masonic since he entitled it as such. He could have chosen not to reveal it as such, since the work is not overtly Masonic. In order to recognize its Masonic character, we would have to look further for proof than we do today in recognizing the same character in the Adagios (K. 410 and K. 411). This work, purely Masonic, remains an invaluable reference point in understanding the influence of symbolism in Mozart's works. The Funeral Ode in fact contains, as a source of inspiration, a number of symbols that we have highlighted and studied above. It is still the most incontestable proof of Mozart's use of the symbols that his initiation had revealed to him.

The three points figure in the key signature as three flats, the work being in C minor and presenting midway, for about twenty measures, a song in E flat major. Einstein and Autexier claim that the total number of measures, sixty-nine, is a symbolic number, but there is nothing Masonic that would justify such an interpretation.

Three calls open the work, neatly inserted in six measures, each one occupying two measures. Three spaces are thus defined and delimited in the writing of the score. Space, as we define it, is what is created between the limits of the responses between the Grand Master and the two Wardens. In its musical writing, the composition opens with the same ritual as that used at the opening of the Masonic work. Moreover, these responses are in thirds, a characteristic symbol of serenity. Then a processional march begins: a real funeral procession, slow and measured, but interrupted by moments of silence (which would be necessary if the piece were only designed to illustrate the ritual of opening or closing the Masonic work). The scope of the composition, the rigor of its writing, and the richness of its orchestration mean that it is a work destined for more than just these moments. In November, Mozart reworked the July score in order to enrich its orchestration. In its original form, the Funeral Ode was less dramatic and ceremonial, not having been designed for public presentation, unlike what would be required by the funeral ceremonies in November.

What then was its real purpose? It is a serious piece of music that undoubtedly accompanies a ritual march. Marches in the Lodge, with specific meanings, are of two types. The first are slow marches by which the brothers who are in charge proceed at the opening and closing of the Masonic work. Others are an integral part of the ceremonies specific to each elevation in Masonic degree and are therefore of a definitely much deeper symbolic meaning.

Mozart had already composed the song "Fellowcraft's Journey" (K. 468) the previous spring for the initiation of his father to the second degree. With the Funeral Ode, he reveals to us another march, this time performed in the course of the ceremony of elevation to the degree of Master, in which the brothers march around the body of King Hiram. It is characterized by its dramatic majesty, and its playing time may correspond to the duration of the procession. This part of the ceremony is not interrupted by any commentary that would require a pause in the melodic line. There is simply a moment of silent meditation on death. But the real symbolism of this third degree is not limited to death alone but, on the contrary, to the rebirth and resurrection which follow it. Death must be evoked, but only to justify a new life. This piece ends with a resplendent major chord, symbolizing rebirth and the joy that accompanies it. Commentators are often astonished by such a resolution in the light. However, this is easily explained: the chord of light draws its evocative power from the contrast with the anguished darkness of death that leads up to it. In the ritual of the third degree, at the end of the ceremony, life and light are conferred upon the initiate. Moreover, in this masterpiece, Mozart translates the feelings that he experiences and, using a symbolic evocation that is perfectly clear to initiates, he relates to us his own vision of death and the Beyond.

Written in July 1785, the Funeral Ode reveals to us what Mozart would confide to his father in his letter of April 4, 1787: "And I offer thanks to my God for having afforded me the good fortune of grasping the opportunity (you understand me) of learning to become acquainted with the key of our true happiness." We need to keep this letter in mind when listening to the Funeral Ode. The vision of death has perhaps never before been expressed and lived with such sincerity: "Death, our true happiness." Holding each day to his vision of death, Mozart spoke of it simply and without anguish; his Masonic belief and faith transcended it in the light and resurrection that the ritual of the degree of Master mason brought to life in the initiate and that the final resplendent chord of hope proclaimed in the Funeral Ode.

Part 2

The Great Works Inspired by Symbolism

Introduction

It is not our concern to analyze the value of these works or bring an esthetic judgment to them. The commentaries on these compositions, which are among some of Mozart's most famous, are so numerous that it seems useless to formulate new ones. Our approach will be limited to discovering in them the inspiration whose source resides in the symbolism that Mozart truly lived in his initiation and later in the practice of his life as a freemason.

Mozart did not compose the great works inspired by symbolism in a systematic fashion during the last seven years of his life. They are situated at precise and limited periods of time. Musicologists see in Mozart's life a series of periods of tension followed by periods of depression as an explanation of the intensity of creation followed by release. We will take this same approach into consideration when assessing the extent of the presence of Masonic thought in his life. It is straightforward to note that the periods of material difficulty are clearly linked to a marked return to the brotherhood. These works reflect his anguish as a man as much as his hope as an initiate.

There are essentially three periods when freemasonry strongly marked Mozart's life, an influence that we find in works composed at these times: The first period covers the year 1785; the second period extends from the spring to the end of the summer of 1788; and the third period covers the twelve months that preceded his death in December 1791.

The first period begins immediately after his initiation on December 14, 1784. Mozart was in regular attendance at various Vienna Lodges as well as his own. His enthusiasm reflected his complete satisfaction at having been received among his brothers. In addition to the ritual compositions from this period, which are included in the List (K. 468, 471, 477, and 484), we can identify the following works directly inspired by Masonic symbolism: the Quartet in A major (K. 464), the Quartet in C major (K. 465), the Concerto for Piano in D minor (K. 466), and the Concerto for Piano in E flat major (K. 482). The Funeral Ode belongs to this period as well, and in the previous chapter we identified the importance of the light it sheds on the real meaning of Masonic compositions.

The second period, March to October 1788, was deeply troubled. At this time, Mozart, having lost his public, was in need of money. He was in mourning at once again losing a child; his daughter, only a few weeks old, died at the end of June. Desperate, he begged the assistance of his brother Michael Puchberg, whom he had known for a long time and who had always supported him. Correspondence from these months reflects Wolfgang's distress. We might think that Puchberg replied too modestly to his urgent appeals. But we must remember that it was Puchberg who always helped him, right up to November 1791. Mozart turned above all to his belief in freemasonry for spiritual comfort and certainty. The inspiration in his musical production shows us that he found both of these.

This second period contains no ritual compositions, but the works inspired by symbolism are the last symphonies: No. 39 in E flat major (K. 543), No. 40 in G minor (K. 550), and No. 41 in C major, the "Jupiter" (K. 551), as well as the Divertimento in E flat major, the "Puchberg Trio" (K. 563).

The third period is the twelve months leading up to his death. As in the two preceding periods, it was a time of intense production. Mozart's need to compose semed to arise from his need to represent the ideals he had acquired since December 1784. The vision that his initiation gave him of the world and the destiny of man is reflected in the equilibrium and harmony of the music of this period. In his last year, the works inspired by freemasonry became more numerous but also reflected a vaster scale. It was almost as a provocation that Mozart openly declared himself a freemason in 1791. If he composed works that carried a message that was not expressed overtly, such as the Quintets for Strings (K. 593 and K. 614), he also composed openly explicitly Masonic cantatas for the public, as he had never done before. We are now very far from the ritual works of 1785 destined only for ceremonies in the Lodge. In this category we find the Little German Cantata "You Who Revere the Creator of the Boundless Universe" (K. 619), the Little Masonic Cantata "Loudly Proclaim Our Joy" (K. 623), followed by the Masonic Song "Let Us Join Our Hands" (K. 623a), and, above all, *The Magic Flute* (K. 620).

6

The First Period: 1785

QUARTET IN A MAJOR (K. 464)

This quartet, written January 10, 1785, is the fifth in the series that Mozart dedicated to Haydn, but it is also the first work written after his initiation. He does not use a precise symbol in this piece. Rather, it renders the overall impression left by his initiation: the rigor, order, and beauty required by the construction of the temple—the Temple in man. His rigor in writing is so evident that one commentator has described it as the musical equivalent of Kant's *Critique of Pure Reason*. Beethoven, who saw in it a perfect masterpiece of structure and harmony, made a copy of the last movement in his own hand.

We are not saying that Mozart had to become a freemason in order to write a work in which rigor was a characteristic of its construction. Rather, we are simply saying that the works written immediately after his initiation could not but bear witness to its importance. This quartet does not incorporate a particular symbol, much less a definite aspect of the initiation; this will be the role of *The Magic Flute*. Its rigor translates order and beauty, the two necessary aspects of the ritual intended to bring the sacred into the Lodge's ceremonies.

The static, almost cold, musical structure is to this quartet what the Doric order is to architecture. The presence of three points in the key signature, in this case three sharps (in this respect Mozart did not see any difference between sharps and flats), would be enough to characterize the work and draw our attention to it. The theme of the first movement is in itself already revealing. It is composed of a query from the first violin and a response by four instruments. (The Massins saw in this writing a representation of the dialogue that would be established in the course of an initiation. But in fact it is *The Magic Flute* that in its totality gives us the representation of this dialogue, with all the intensity that it implies, between the Priest and Tamino.) If there is actually a dialogue, it seems to be limited to the exchange of words between the Grand Master and the Wardens at the moment of the opening or closing of the work of the Lodge. Indeed, the simplicity of the writing does not seem adequate, and as a result not convincing enough, to allow such an evocation of initiation.

It should be said, however, that in the last movement an indisputable symbolic meaning accompanies the introduction of a chorale that appears after an astonishing silence. In music, the chorale is the actual expression of rigor or structure—or better still, of constructive reflection. This insertion is the most meaningful element of the quartet and is indeed its most Masonic moment. Mozart invokes the chorale in compositions that are influenced by the symbol of rigor and seriousness: the Funeral Ode and the chorale of the two armed men in *The Magic Flute*, a chorale that happens at the very moment of the initiation of the postulants. We can connect the chorale of this quartet and that of *The Magic Flute*. Both have an identical evocative power; both remind us, spanning an interval of six years, of Mozart's initiation and that of Tamino.

QUARTET IN C MAJOR (K. 465)

On January 14, 1785, four days after the composition of the previous quartet, Mozart completed the sixth and last quartet of the series dedicated to Haydn. After hearing these two works, Haydn declared to Leopold that Wolfgang was the greatest composer that the world had ever known.

The short time between the composition of these two quartets explains their total similarity of inspiration. Whereas rigor characterizes the previous quartet, clarity characterizes this one. If the influence of Masonic thought, although definite, was only shown partially in the first quartet, it is incontrovertible in the second, being so apparent.

This quartet on clarity is known, surprisingly, as "Dissonance." In reality there is no incoherence or incompatibility. Its first movement is made up of two very distinct parts: the first, a slow introduction of difficult composition, stumbling to the point of seeming badly written and dissonant; the second, following immediately, the main theme of the greatest purity and clarity. This work brings Masonic symbols into high relief. We could in fact wonder if, given the date of its composition, it was not the first work entrusted to Mozart as an Entered Apprentice. It could have been, we might say, his first "paper" (the term used for a presentation by a brother in the Lodge). This is only a speculation but it is quite possible when we consider the importance of the work that any newly initiated brother, by regulation, has to accomplish—a regulation to which Mozart would have been subjected.

This concerto is based on the use of one symbol only—that of attaining to the light—but undertaken with creative force and exceptional mastery of composition. Contrary to what some commentators have stated, light is revealed to the freemason starting with his initiation to the first degree—that of Entered Apprentice. Of course, light can be conferred again, according to the various rites, in the course of initiatory ceremonies marking his rising in the Order. Be that as it may, the revelation of light is a fundamental element in the first initiation; in fact, it is its main point. One can understand that Mozart was struck by the emotional power of the ceremony and this symbol, and saw in them the underlying foundation of his new Masonic belief. From this moment forward, Mozart wished us to perceive this symbol's grandeur, thereby sharing with us the joy he experienced in living through the initiation, which was providing a new direction to his life.

The Quartet in C thus symbolizes the passage from darkness to the light. Darkness is expressed by the opacity of the musical writing, dark harmonies, and the use of dissonances, which the musicologists of the classic period considered incredible mistakes, and which gave this quartet its name.

The musical translation of light results in the appearance of C major through a song of total purity, purity that seems all the more stately since it constitutes a counterpoint to the disturbance that precedes it.

The attainment of the light proceeds not only from darkness but also through a slow march, an adagio that renders the search even more agonizing. We find that on one other occasion, Mozart uses this primordial symbol in the same kind of writing: when composing the overture to Symphony No. 39 in E flat major (K. 543).

CONCERTO FOR PIANO IN D MINOR, No. 20 (K. 466)

This concerto, dated February 10, 1785, occupies an exceptional place among Mozart's works. It was the only one (noting for opposite reasons Concerto No. 26 in D major, K. 537) whose great scope attracted the attention of nineteenth-century pianists. Beethoven, who appreciated it most particularly, composed a cadenza for it. The English musicologist C. M. Girdlestone, in his analysis of Mozart's concertos, writes: "We leap at one bound from one world to another totally different. There is no longer any trace of those march or dance rhythms, those opera buffa closes, those good-humouredly symmetrical strains."[1] This judgment seems unfair and above all pointlessly severe for the works that precede the Concerto in D major, but he is accurate in emphasizing a break from them. To us, this break does not seem to necessarily isolate this concerto from those before it, but rather to ascribe to it a different character, just as the Quartet in A (K. 464) was itself different from its predecessors in the series dedicated to Haydn. Jean-Victor Hocquard says, "With this work we seem to move from the eighteenth to the nineteenth century."[2] This comment has the advantage of explaining why the nineteenth century favored this concerto so much over the others. All the musicologists who have studied it agree that it represents two things: a break and new content.

In order to understand this work, it is necessary to examine all the events of the period of its creation as well as its position in the series of compositions appearing before and after February 10, 1785. In the suite of piano concerti, the concerto preceding the D minor is No. 19 in F major (K. 459), dated December 10, 1784. Mozart himself considered the nineteenth concerto to be of some importance, since we know that he performed it in Leipzig in 1789. There is no point in looking for a break in the musical quality of these two compositions; on the contrary, the quality is completely sustained.

Two works precede the D minor concerto by only a few days, but both follow Mozart's initiation; they are in fact the two string quartets that we have just examined.

The work that follows Concerto No. 20 by a few days is the Concerto No. 21 in C major (K. 467); it is without any Masonic characteristics. The progression of the compositions during the first three months of 1785 leads us to believe that, if there is a break, it is not in the sense that musicologists generally understand the term.

There would have been a real break if the works following Concerto No. 20, therefore after February 10, were of an inspiration and a quality of writing that was different from the preceding concerti. There would have been a break if Concerto No. 21 no longer showed qualities that it shared with Concerto No. 19. However, this is not at all the case. Concerti Nos. 19 and 21 are similar in writing and identical in spirit; they express a similar gaiety and poetry in their songs and simple melodic lines. Concerto No. 20, therefore, does not bring to a close the "eighteenth-century style," since this style remains the most noticeable characteristic of the following concerto.

If there is no real break, there is, however, new content. The Masonic inspiration that we highlighted in the A and C quartets (K. 464 and K. 465) are also found in this concerto. The new content is no doubt the result of deep reflection inspired in Mozart by his recent initiation.

The documentary record shows that the life of the new initiate during late 1784–early 1785 seems to have been devoted to his Masonic activities (see Appendix 2). Mozart composed with great intensity, animated with a neophyte's fire, bearing witness to his new convictions.

The Concerto in D minor draws on this source of inspiration. Its expression is necessarily broader and more imposing than that of the two quartets of January. Mozart knew that through the orchestra he was addressing a large public with whom he shared his vision. His care in expressing his current concern, his new hope, constituted the actual new content.

The first three bars of the *allegro* of the first movement refer to the symbol of the steps leading to the entrance of the temple—a movement of elevation—sketched by the cellos and double basses, while the violins and violas repeat a single note. Such a form of writing excludes any melodic line, creating however a heavy atmosphere, similar to the dusk into which the composer wishes the listener to be plunged. This musical dusk is quite appropriate in evoking a thoughtfulness that must of necessity lead to clarity through initiation.

For the first time, Mozart drew on the symbol of steps. He would have recourse to it again to show us that his gaze and his mind had turned toward the dawn. The last symphonies also carry the message of hope. This symbol, laden with more meaning every day for Mozart, reappears in the first bars of both Symphony

No. 38, "Prague" (K. 504), and Symphony No. 41, "Jupiter" (K. 551). In the Concerto in D minor, which is issued as the first great orchestral work inspired by the symbol, Mozart wielded his musical transcription.

Starting from the first notes, the work establishes itself as would a Masonic ceremony. The responses between the strings and the woodwinds illustrate the responses of the ritual, using ascending chords whose structure extends the concept. These responses continue this way until the bassoons and the oboes softly express an E flat major chord. This chord is not expressly characterized by its force any more than is the musical line in C major, which sketches the initial theme of the "Dissonances" Quartet. If it is discreet, it is however indicative of the transition operating in the harmony between the profane and the sacred.

In this first movement, the piano's theme continues to be astonishingly distinct from that of the orchestra. It remains a questioning song, even more luminous for the fact that the orchestra maintains a heavy zone of shadow. Contrary to what Girdlestone says, nothing in this movement is to be thought of as a "relentless struggle, a piling and speeding up instead of alternation."[3] The serene reflection entrusted to the piano remains independent, as if remaining above the passions conveyed by the orchestra. The first movement ends with a return to the initial motif of steps, using a form identical to that used at the beginning. But whereas the expression at the beginning was violent and peremptory, it is all softness and calm in the final bars. The day, born at the start of the work as it arrives in the Orient, has illuminated, through the allegro, the heavens of its fulfillment.

Serenity has been won, translated by the first notes of the second movement and impregnated with the calm of the *romanze* sung first of all by the piano alone. The orchestra then picks it up and a conversation of hushed quality starts up between orchestra and solo instrument. There is no evidence of another symbol in this movement, which remains fully illuminated with Masonic clarity.

In addition, the surprising break that intervenes in the middle of this elegiac romance, like a storm that strikes without warning, astonishes by its savagery. Mozart seemed to want to tell us of the fragility of happiness. This contrast, expressed with such brutality, shares the yin and the yang of Masonic morality: for example, the opposition of night and day or good and evil. In reference to the symbolism, it would be impossible, either musically or logically, for the second movement to end with this violence. So the theme of romance again makes itself heard, even more movingly, and returns the movement to its initial serenity at the close.

The third movement is a very quick *allegro* that begins, like the second movement, with a piano solo of surprising vehemence. It is not possible to consider it, as Girdlestone would have it, "a conflict that is even wilder than that inspired by the first movement." We don't see how the writing and the tempo would render this third movement tense and combative. Hocquard quite rightly sees in it "a vibrant and self-assured energy: the spirit of Tamino." Without defining the implication and the consequence of a connection between the spirit of this concerto and the symbolic reference to Tamino, Hocquard is certainly right in drawing our attention to the piece in which Mozart sings of his faith as an initiate.

The last movement concludes with a joyful and important coda in a major key. This ending has given rise to the most divergent views. Quite a few people have seen it simply as an expression of Mozart's friendly concern toward his listeners, as if it would be unseemly to leave them with an impression that the concerto was unresolved dramatically. Others have taken it purely as an esthetic need on Mozart's part to intersperse the end of the movement with moments of joyful relaxation. In fact, this concerto could conclude in no other way than with joy, expressed by the wind instruments. It seems to have been composed only to tell us that joy must remain in our hearts, just as the text of the ritual would have it. From the beginning, this work would have obliged the listener to lead his spirit toward a true ascension and would have called him to raise himself above his own human condition, through a meditation on the content of the symbols.

Recognizing the nature of the inspiration through an analysis of the symbolism allows us to confirm the opinion of authors who have perceived the dynamism of this "ascent," even though they might not have been able to give a reason or justification for it. Hocquard speaks of a "triumphal outburst that is the culmination of the continuous ascent and the natural result of an heroic break-through. Then led by the woodwinds into a quiet light, we have the beautiful major theme. The piano picks it up with rapture and complete clarity." Except for the fact that it is hard to see both a "triumphant outburst" and a "quiet light" in the same theme, we need to recognize that Hocquard has evoked the culmination of the continuous ascent toward the light. We know that this theme in a major key, which has caught his attention, is nothing less than the musical transcription of the symbol of light revealed to the initiate that we have already discussed in regard to the Funeral Ode and the "Dissonance" Quartet. Jean and Brigitte Massin were not able "to believe that it could be by chance that, on the day after his entry into freemasonry, the human vision of Mozart's music increases in its scope while, at the same time, its expression becomes, not less, but ever more personal." They are right: it is not through chance that this concerto corresponds to personal inner reflection. It is very clearly a work that reflects the deep convictions and new knowledge that Mozart had acquired through his recent practice of the Royal Art.

CONCERTO FOR PIANO IN E FLAT MAJOR, NO. 22 (K. 482)

This concerto is dated December 6, 1785. Most musicologists see in it a return to the past. Hocquard speaks of "a work that is in a way a historical summary. It would seem that Mozart is trying to express the states that he has passed through since his childhood and, that by doing so, he is not taking refuge in nostalgia for his past but rather is engaging, for the present and for the future, in a taking stock." C. M. Girdlestone notes, "From the earliest days of his life as a composer, there is heard an ideal song which the child, and then the youth, tries to reproduce. He has rendered it once for all in its perfection in this concerto." The Massins, referring to the concerto that Mozart had composed in 1777 ("Jeunhomme," K. 271), wrote, "After almost nine years, and full of the experience of those years, Mozart returns to the initial music from his twenty-first year."

From our point of view, we see no reason to reach back so far into the past. Concerto No. 22 is not a re-expression of either Wolfgang's childhood or his adolescence. It quite clearly reflects his recent initiation. If it seems accurate to see in this piece a return to the past, it is a return only to December 14, 1784, with, as we know, the more precise and significant meaning of that date. We cannot go far wrong in considering Concerto No. 22 the one that Mozart wanted to compose for the anniversary of his initiation. The piece was not performed at the Lodge, but Mozart no doubt let his freemason friends know the reasons behind its composition.

December 1785 was a period in which the Masonic works played a fundamental role. Mozart, as he had done in the spring, overtly wrote officially Masonic works for special occasions: the two chorales (K. 483 and K. 484) for the inauguration of the "New Hope Crowned" Lodge, and especially the two adagios for wind instruments (K. 410 and K. 411). Concerning these two latter works, which are fundamental to understanding the totality of Mozart's Masonic compositions, we should mention that it would be a mistake to fix a date for them earlier than December 1784. Given the initiatory knowledge that they reflect and the rigor of their composition, they could not have been composed while Mozart was still a layman.

The first half of 1785 had been an intensely creative period for Mozart, from immediately after his initiation to the composition of the Funeral Ode in July. He delighted in proclaiming his new convictions with pleasure and insistence. That December, after a barren summer and autumn, appears to have been a time of return to works of a Masonic character. Concerto No. 22 is one of the most significant of this period.

The dazzling bars that open this concerto have led it to be called the most "royal" of all his works. This description is based on the belief that Mozart wanted to interest his Viennese public more and attract them through brilliant (if not necessarily easier) writing. To demonstrate the inaccuracy of this opinion, we need only recall that it was not the work as a whole that attracted the public, but more particularly the *andante* of the second movement, which is marked by a previously unknown melancholy, sadness, and depth. Leopold, who was present at its performance, told his daughter that Wolfgang had to perform an encore of the second movement, which was, he took the trouble to stress, exceptional. In fact, what was exceptional was not so much that the second movement should be performed again as that this *andante* with its apparently infinite sadness was acclaimed by the public.

The work is written in E flat major. As it happens, the use of this key signifies the desire to intentionally express the presence of symbolism. Indeed, Mozart deliberately kept the three points in the key signature for the tonality of the three movements. This second movement, whose force and spiritual elevation are the concerto's raison d'être, is in the same key as the Funeral Ode. Within a six-month interval, the second movement of this concerto reprises the spirit of the symbolic composition that characterized the third degree: that of Master mason.

The Massins went further in the interpretation that they ascribed to the presence of E flat major in Concerto No. 22. This concerto is the first of three composed, over a very brief period, for the winter performance season of 1785–1786. It is remarkable that the tonality of each of these three concerti requires the presence of three points in the key signature: No. 22 (K. 482) in E flat major (three flats), No. 23 (K. 488) in A major (three sharps), and No. 23 (K. 491) in C minor (three flats). For these musicologists, the three concerti were equally inspired by the same symbolic thought and they constitute a triptych, having been composed "jointly," with an astonishing attention to their similarity in the choice of tonalities determined by the marking of three points. This hypothesis deserves consideration. But in our view, the idea of a Masonic triptych does not seem to be justified. The presence of the symbol of three signature points in concerti No. 23 and 24 is not clear. As we shall see, the three last symphonies (Nos. 39–41) constitute, par excellence, such a triptych, since during their twelve total movements, Mozart repeatedly uses several symbols, which are really connecting threads through the three works. In contrast, Concertos No. 23 and No. 24 contain no Masonic symbolism that would lead us to think that they are extensions of Concerto No. 22.

The ambiance of this *andante*, which deserves our attention, differs from that of the *andante* in Concerto No. 20, which was totally elegiac. The latter *andante* offers a vision of perfect melancholy and of meditation on the Beyond. The closeness between these two concerti, both of Masonic inspiration, allows us to bring out interesting aspects that result from contrasting the tonalities in their different movements.

Concerto No. 20 (K. 466) D minor	Concerto No. 22 (K. 482) E flat major
First movement: quick minor.	First movement: quick major.
Second movement: slow major, with insertion of quick minor (symbol of opposition).	Second movement: slow minor, with insertion of major (symbol of opposition).
Third movement: quick minor.	Third movement: quick major, with slow major insertion.

The theme of this second movement appears three times on the piano in the form of variations supported by an imperceptible accompaniment of chords. During these three variations, reintroduced intentionally in the same key of C minor, the wind instruments come in the first time in E flat major, the second time in C major, and the third time in the coda. The line on the piano is then interwoven with the whole orchestra. In this coda, Girdlestone sees one of the most marvelous moments in all of Mozart. The opposition among the instruments does not lead one to infer violent combat, but rather a truly intense dialogue between the piano and the wind instruments, expressing the deepening of Mozart's meditation. At no time does it lead to despair or revolt. To the anxious questioning of the piano, the wind instruments respond with serenity; each of their responses is the very expression of calm and certitude. The second response of the wind instruments is notably marked by the almost joyful intervention of the flute. Thus, in this passage, there now appears the instrument that six years later will have an identical symbolic function in the opera.

Hocquard's analysis repeatedly connects this *andante* with *The Magic Flute*. The dialogue is, for him, that of Tamino asking for entry to the Temple. If combat in the opposition between the musical themes is to be seen, it is that waged against the temptations, which will be vanquished by the wisdom of the initiate. Hocquard sees in the conclusion of the coda the same "aurora" as the one that illuminates the resolution of the Funeral Ode.

We mention this analysis, which highlights the similarity in character between the two works, even though it does not explain Mozart's recourse to the content of the symbols that constitute the real justification for their similarity.

This meditation, which is the heart of the *andante* and which concludes in the luminous grandeur of its coda, shows us once again Mozart's precise vision of the Beyond. Moreover, the piece culminates with three symbolic "knocks," clearly and simply expressed in thirds by the whole of the orchestra, just like a veritable closing of the Lodge.

Our attention should focus on the presence of the wind instruments and especially on the importance of their role and meaning.

Mozart entrusted the care of expressing serenity to them, just as he did in the Funeral Ode. Moreover, the melodic line, using an intentionally simple structure, recalls in its amplitude the structure of the Adagio (K. 411). We have seen that this adagio is actually a movement with a processional character that can accompany a ritual march in the Lodge; such a march was always associated with bringing the sacred to the assembly. It is not surprising that Mozart, who wanted to bestow a meditative force on the *andante* of Concerto No. 22, would make a connection to this work that is marked by its expression of liturgical contemplation. This relationship, in reference to the spirit and inspiration of the adagio and the concerto, would tend to confirm the opinion that the dates of composition of these two works are not far apart.

The four significant notes that will outline one of these themes in the last movement of Symphony No. 41 in C major (K. 551) already appear in this concerto. Here we once again have proof of the undeniable influence between Mozart's works of symbolic inspiration.

It is also quite startling to notice, in the third and last movement of this concerto, the melodic line that Mozart will use once again for the toast in the second act of *Così Fan Tutte*. This theme, characterized by its sweetness of melody and slowness of rhythm, enters as an unexpected break in the joyful exuberance of this movement. This surprising insertion, imbued with certitude and calm, is just as astonishing as the insertion we have already encountered in the second movement of Concerto No. 20. You will recall that, in the latter concerto, the unexpected shock of violence breaks into the elegiac melody. In contrast, in Concerto No. 22, when Mozart intends to express a simple happiness, an equally unexpected moment of serenity breaks in to soften what would otherwise be an excess of gaiety. So, might we not consider the toast, which takes place in the midst of the everyday, bubbling lightness of the final passage of *Così*, to be the sublimated desire of the belief in happiness expressed using symbolic musical language?

7

The Second Period: 1788

In the previous chapter, we saw the exaltation of the newly initiated Mozart as well as his desire to express the results of his spiritual inquiry using explorations of musical forms. In this period, we see the appearance of works no less exceptional in scope in which Mozart proclaimed even more forcefully his reasons for hope even while he was painfully constrained by personal troubles.

This period, like the first in 1785 and the third in 1791, is characterized by an intensity of production that is hard to imagine. It is noteworthy to review the list of these compositions. It proves that once Mozart decided to write, nothing stood in his way, regardless of the size of the material, physical, or moral obstacle. The summer of 1788 is certainly one of his most painful periods but is nevertheless one of the most productive.

June 26: Trio for piano, violin, and cello in E major (K. 542).
June 26: Symphony No. 39 in E flat major (K. 543).
June 26: March in D major (K. 544).

June 26: Sonata for piano in C major, "Easy" (K. 545).

June 26: Adagio and fugue for strings in C minor (K. 546).

July 10: Sonata for violin and piano in F major (K. 547).

July 14: Trio for piano, violin, and cello in C major (K. 548).

July 16: Conzonetta "Piu non si trovano" (K. 549).

July 25: Sympony No. 40 in G minor (K. 550).

August 10: Symphony No. 41 in C major, "Jupiter" (K. 551).

August 11: Lied "Dem hohen Kaiser Wort treu" (K. 552).

September 2: Ten Canons (K. 553 to K. 562) (entered on this date but composed earlier).

September 27: Divertimento for viola and cello in E flat major, "Puchberg Trio" (K. 563).

We fix the beginning of this period in March. From spring-time onward, Mozart understood and expressed his adversity. *Don Juan* enjoyed some success—but in Prague, not in Vienna. Friedrich Rochlitz, editor of a contemporary music journal, reported that, at a salon, Viennese high society quibbled about the real value of this opera. Haydn intervened to declare, "All I know is that Mozart is the greatest composer in the world today." But Haydn's opinion alone was not enough for Mozart's genius to be fully accepted. He sank deeper and deeper into misery.

The Adagio for piano in B minor (K. 540), from March, tells us what Mozart was really feeling then. What specific reason would he have had to confide in us something so painful, which he had not done until this point? We will never know. And yet we really ought to think of this adagio not as a simple musical work but as a baring of Mozart's heart, exceptional among all his composi-tions. It is perhaps the only one we have in which he expresses unreservedly his deepest feelings and his most intimate and painful thoughts. He wrote this work for solo piano, not to have it performed in public, but rather in order that the pianist playing it, in his solitude and outside time, might forever remain the confidant of the composer's distress.

The last symphonies

The following symphonies are Mozart's last:

- No. 39 in E flat major (K. 543), June 1788
- No. 40 in G minor (K. 550), July 1788
- No. 41 in C major (K. 551), August 1788

Our study of these symphonies will be limited to discovering in them the expression of Mozart's Masonic beliefs. The creation of these works provided him with moral support in a period of profound despair.

Because they happen to be the last ones written, they are seen as his final statement and legacy. What an astonishing presumption! In 1788, why would Mozart be so sure of his "imminent death" (three years later) that he would hasten to create three symphonies in order to make them into a farewell message? As noted by Jean and Brigitte Massin, it is both more serious and touching that "these symphonies are the last because if they had been a success, Mozart would have written others. He wrote them to make the voice of his heart heard and once he understood that no one was listening, he fell silent."

Musicologists have wondered if these three symphonies form a trilogy or triptych. They don't seem to have been written for the musical season of the winter of 1788–1789. Mozart had no assurance that he would be playing them, given the disapproval of the

Viennese public. He certainly would not have undertaken compositions of such magnitude six months in advance. We should recall that the three concerti for piano from the winter season of 1785, intended for performance, were composed only at the end of that fall. Also, if Mozart had thought of these compositions as a possible source of future revenue, he would not have failed to have spoken about them to Puchberg, whom he asked for financial assistance in his letter of June 17, 1788. Mozart alluded to the possibility of music lovers, especially non-Viennese ones, subscribing to future works. If these three symphonies had been written for such a subscription, we can assume that Mozart would have said so, since, in this case, they would have been "under construction" in June. They were composed in an incredibly short space of time—barely two months. In a way, Mozart had all of them in his head at the same time and they matured together. Today, they seem to us like three components of a single vast orchestral composition.

Were they written in the same order as that given in the Köchel catalog? If their order of creation were different from that implied by their catalog dates, could this indicate an actual intention we know nothing about? Alfred Einstein, who asks this question, doesn't think so. Nevertheless he shows that they really form a consistent whole. He even goes so far as to suggest that the components are interchangeable. Hocquard believes that Einstein is right since, in his opinion, there is no logically systematic progression among them.

On the contrary, an analysis based on symbols, as we have continually been doing, makes clear a perfectly logical unfolding of inspiration throughout these compositions; Mozart recorded them in his catalog according to this logic. Symphony No. 39 in E flat, which opens with an adagio reminiscent of a vast portal symbolizing the opening of work in the Lodge and the convey-ance of the sacred to this work, can only have been the first of the three. Similarly, the fugue that characterizes the last move-ment of Symphony No. 41 shows clearly that this symphony is the last of the three because its musical expression portrays the symbol of the temple's construction being completed in order and beauty. Symphony No. 40 in G minor thus comes in the middle. Moreover, that is logically where it should be, since it symbolizes the difficulties to be overcome in the necessary passage through the coherent unfolding of these three works.

SYMPHONY NO. 39
IN E FLAT MAJOR (K. 543)

In studying this symphony, we have been unable to establish a suitable connection between, on the one hand, the adagio that pre-cedes the theme of its first movement and, on the other hand, the adagio that precedes the theme of the "Dissonance" Quartet in C major (K. 465). Yet the similarity in composition and musical language is clear.

Our previous analysis of the C major quartet is applicable here almost in its entirety. In both cases it is a question of the passage from the secular world to the sacred, from chaos to order.

The symbol of the three signature points of E flat major is clear, as it was for Concerto No. 22. This tonality colors the whole of the trilogy.

The first six bars indicate the Masonic character of this work. Except for an isolated first chord, the strings ritually delineate three times three beats. They foreshadow those at the opening of

The Magic Flute and are a sign of the similarity in conception and inspiration between these works. However, the nine "knocks" are not expressed free of interruption; each group of three is followed by a descending scale lacking in ornamentation and orchestration, ending with a chord that is part of the scale and not one of the beats. So the spelling out of the beats remains unadulterated. These scales play the important role of introducing at the beginning the symbol of space from which the work as a whole will derive its source of inspiration.

Even though the rigor of the writing almost makes them expressive, the nature of these two symbols (triple beats and space) is in no way illustrative or descriptive. These symbols are there for their meaning, not their formal, external aspect.

Thus, as with the "Dissonance" Quartet, darkness weighs heavily within this introduction, created precisely by the obsessive rhythm and the absence of harmony in the writing. The adagio moves forward in slow and heavy steps without introducing a real theme. Then, ten bars before the end, the impression changes completely. Three scales, ascending this time, replace those that until this point have been descending. The ternary rhythm of darkness dissipates little by little as the day breaks. The tempo slows down and a few notes, in great simplicity, evoke the horizon where the light will rise.

From this point on, the clarity of the musical line making up the theme of the first movement replaces the harmonies of darkness in the overture. If we wanted to single out this symphony, we could quite justifiably name it "Symphony of the Dawn."

It would seem that nowhere else in any music is there a comparable theme, so simple and perfect, able to become, in its spareness and transparency, light itself. This theme is elaborated in a series of notes using thirds, an interval whose symbolic character Mozart used to represent fulfillment and serenity.

Using such an introductory adagio is not unusual. We should recall that Haydn used it in exactly the same way for his Parisian Masonic symphonies. But only Wolfgang, through the breadth of his writing and his vision of this symbol, has been able to portray daybreak using musical harmony.

Thus the listener is led, without knowing it, to the world that an initiate can reach. In the first measures of Symphony No. 39, Einstein quite rightly sees Tamino knocking at the door of the Temple. His insight allows us to say that while commentators have not looked for the real inspiration of these symphonies, they have unconsciously and quite rightly grasped their symbolic character.

The second movement, in A flat major, is marked by a statement and responses which, like the alternating black and white squares in the mosaic tiles of the Lodge's floor, symbolize space. This symbol seems to convey from the beginning of the symphony the need to hold the listener within "sanctified" musical space; maintaining the sacred space uninterrupted is in fact necessary to sustain the total serenity of the piece. Moving in his imagination from one musical motif to another, the listener himself creates this space and proceeds through it in his mind. This second movement advances through an expanse that is vast and calm, as if the rising up of the music remains all the more simple and pure in tracing the line of an invisible horizon.

SYMPHONY NO. 40 IN G MINOR (K. 550)

The Symphony in G minor has given rise to commentaries that are overdrawn and contradictory. "This symphony has nothing striking about it, either in its interventions (?), or in its elaboration; it's an ordinary piece of sweet music" (Hermann Hirschbach). "*Joie de vivre*" (C. Palmer). "Lighthearted minuet" (Hector Berlioz). "Soaring Hellenic grace" (Robert Schumann). In other commentators, it inspires a totally different view: "It constitutes the most biting manifestation of a deeply pessimistic fatalism, which . . . attempts to surface in his art" (H. Albert). "It's an uncharacteristic outburst transformed into brilliant excesses" (Georges de Saint-Foix).

Between the previous symphony, illuminated by a nascent clarity, and the following one, bathed in dazzling light, Mozart seems to have wanted to make Symphony No. 40 a symphony of half-light. It accentuates a contrast in which the symbolic value is very clear (and which confirms the unique inspiration of these three last symphonies). In speaking of this symphony, we should restate the essentially initiatory value of the symbol of opposition or opposites, such as fire and water, heaven and earth, darkness and light. Mozart had already shown, in the works previously studied, that he was well acquainted with the fundamental value of this symbol and knew very well how he could, through the genius of his composition, extend its content.

There is another idea we can see in this symphony: man's return to himself through thought and struggle. In so doing, he understands himself and sees what he must pursue in order to overcome his own weaknesses and temptations. Such contemplation, which leads him to a vision of his own destiny, is one of the sources of inspiration for this complex and elusive symphony. The responses to the unsettling questions that this symphony raises are not found within the symphony itself but rather in the following Symphony, No. 41. The last movement of that symphony conveys the certainty and serenity that Mozart intended the initiate to reach.

This symphony is not a lesson in morality that, in the form of a hymn, would sing of the obligation to construct the Temple in man with wisdom and beauty. It is strongly marked by the necessity of accepting that pain is the unavoidable path toward serenity. We should not then be surprised to find in it the expression of a creative energy, of a willingness to build, whose structure is shown even more clearly through the contrapuntal writing. The complexity of this work, marked not only by anxiety and tension but also by very brief openings to clarity, explains the range of commentaries, whether they notice only the aspect of human suffering, or wish to remember only the delicate intimations of hope that it harbors.

The Symphony in G minor does not express rebellion against the injustice and violence of existence, but rather, with restraint, the anguish of despair. It is one of the most significant works regarding Mozart's reaction to pain, a reaction that excludes any exuberance or outward display. If despair is present, it is kept deep in the heart out of a sense of propriety.

This despair, which Mozart tells us needs to be overcome, ran through the days of June 1788 when the symphony was composed. In a letter addressed to Puchberg, ten days after composing the work, Mozart imparted his distress and once again asked for his friend's help. "Please. Come and see me. I am still at home. In ten days I've gotten through more work than I would have in two months in my former quarters, and if I were not so often prey to dark thoughts, which I manage to dispel with huge difficulty, things would go better . . . I won't take any more of your time with my going on. I'll bring these words to a stop so hope can commence."

The symbol of the beats struck in the first measures points

to the Masonic character of the Symphony in G minor. Three "knocks" are struck three times, very rapidly but ritually. Then they become the integral and harmonic element of the whole first movement. They are repeated seamlessly in clever modulations and in varied forms throughout multiple reintroductions by various instruments of the orchestra. This kind of writing excludes any theme dependent on melody. It is astonishing that this hammering, so clearly spelled out from the very beginning of the work, intentionally belabored in its form, and repeated obsessively, has never been noticed by musicologists. Were they to look, they would find proof of what they might have suspected—a Masonic influence. These nine "knocks" (under whatever form and composition they appear in the ensemble of movements) authenticate the Masonic vision of the symphony. The Massins declared: "Extending beyond an individual lyricism, Mozart more universally addresses all of humanity."

The absence, as in the initial allegro, of a real theme or melodic line similarly characterizes the *andante* of the second movement. Here, the presence of three points in the key signature (flats) once again strongly confirms the persistence of the symbolic character of the three symphonies. Indeed, Mozart could have employed B flat major, a major key related to the initial key of the symphony, which would have been more logical musically. However, the logic is symbolic, not musical. That is why the key of B flat major

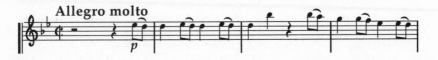

Symphony No. 40 in G minor (K. 550)

could be considered unfortunate since it would have expressed a "different spirit" from that of the triptych. It is clear that, in the course of the composition, Wolfgang deliberately returns to this symbolic key, exemplary of the E flat major which soars over the three symphonies. Using his ternary symbol throughout the work, he reminds us why the work was written.

The tempo of the first movement having calmed, it is natural that the anxious tension characterizing it would also lessen. In the second movement, the ongoing expression of anxiety is entrusted more to the rhythm than to the harmonization. The 6/8 time (for example, in measures 55 and 67) can include six times two eighth notes and a sixteenth rest. This phrasing uses two legato notes, broken by a stop, repeated almost continuously throughout the whole of the movement. It shows Mozart's intention of inexorably employing this same breathless motif—a musical expression of the tension of the search.

Certain authors, following Einstein, consider these legato notes to be a reference to fraternity: masons joining hands in a chain of union. That does not seem to be the case to me. This phrasing, in its rhythm, musically represents the breathlessness of oppression (apparently that of Mozart tortured by dark thoughts, which he dispelled only with difficulty).

The level of veritable superconsciousness to which the work has been raised, supported by the power of symbols, cancels out any expression limited to personal anxiety. Mozart's music belongs to all humanity, for the feelings that it expresses are not only his own. Carried to the spiritual elevation that universal symbols require, the symphony is untainted by petty individualism.

If we were to look for an allusion to fraternity in this second movement, it would be in the dialogue between the wind instruments and the strings. Moreover, these responses play a similar role to that entrusted to the ascending and descending group of triple sixteenth notes; they too define the sacred space set aside for meditation.

Discreetly, a theme of four notes is heard a little later. This theme has particular but definite meaning in this anxious adagio— a glimmer of hope. Indeed, we have here nothing less than the four notes that, having become architectural elements, will be enlarged upon in the construction of the dazzling finale of the following symphony. This insertion of four notes proves once again that the sequence, adopted by Mozart and followed in the Köchel catalog for the three symphonies, is in a logical order. This theme of four notes, briefly and crisply spelled out here, will be deployed in the following symphony. The reverse order would be inconceivable. This proves once again that the Symphony in G minor has to come before Symphony No. 41 in C major since it is in the latter that the theme is developed.

The last two movements, a minuet and a final allegro, following the concentration of the *andante*, recreate the tension of the initial movement. This tension is pushed to the extreme in the final *allegro* without bringing in any new symbol. Having already conveyed his thoughts as an initiate, Mozart no longer needs to reintroduce meaningful symbols in these last two movements. The violence that characterizes the last movement excludes any possibility of a return to calm. Thus, the final chords, although they musically conclude the score, do not provide a response to the questions that constituted the inspiration of the composition. Mozart entrusts this role to the last symphony, the one called "Jupiter."

SYMPHONY NO. 41 IN C MAJOR, "JUPITER" (K. 551)

The "Jupiter" symphony is the last of the trilogy, intended to speak of the accomplishment of the initiatory process.

In the Lodge, the freemason keeps his eyes turned toward the throne of King Solomon where the Grand Master is seated, just above the three steps. From this place, the Orient, the Master must enlighten his brothers and guide them in their work, as the sun illuminates the day.

With the first bars of Symphony No. 41, Mozart symbolically places the listener at the foot of the altar, facing these three steps. We have already seen this meaning in Concerto No. 20 in D minor. And we find it once again, used in an identical fashion and with the same symbolic value, at the beginning of Symphony No. 38 in D major, "Prague."

(We should recall that Mozart composed Symphony No. 38 in December 1786 as he prepared for a trip to Prague where he had been invited by freemason friends. Once again, we see here a work composed in recognition of the fraternity. We haven't studied this symphony in detail even though we know that it is clearly a work of Masonic inspiration. We will limit our comment to saying that it contains symbols with which we are familiar, such as the introductory adagio which leads from darkness to the light, rhythms of breathlessness, and the presence of steps leading to the Orient.)

In Symphony No. 41, Mozart places the listener at the foot of the altar, in a situation identical to that of the initiate in the Lodge.

These three steps, as in the earlier works, are transcribed by ascending triplets, "trills running into the tonic." The tonic plays an essential role in the first movement of the symphony. It rings three times; a violent dynamic arises from it, all the more strongly expressed by the instruments coming together. This affirming motif (if we can speak of a motif when it is so short) is immediately followed by a questioning theme that ends on a fourth. Thus, in only four bars, Mozart has reintroduced a symbol, that of space, which is created by the alternation of motifs: strength and tenderness, masculine and feminine. Using a more concise statement and a harmonic that is shorter but identical, Mozart returns in the beginning of this symphony to what he had already expressed in the *andante* of Symphony No. 39. This confirms the unity of inspiration in the three last symphonies.

Right from its first movement, this symphony extends the preceding symphony but, above all, resolves the concerns that it had expressed. Passion and anxiety are now overcome. A symphony of equilibrium and order; a veritable architecture that Mozart creates based on his convictions and himself; a symphony whose greatness is simply the reflection of an ideal; a symphony of fulfillment in which scarcely does a musical motif appear before the calm response of certitude replies: such is the "Jupiter" symphony.

The serene dialogue of the second movement, an *andante cantabile*, is deliberately different from the second movement of Symphony No. 40. It is not touched by any anxiety or any darkness. Without letting up but without tension, the score moves the listener toward full light, just as Tamino will move toward the light of his initiation.

To understand the unity of thought in the trilogy, we need to connect the last movement of the "Jupiter" symphony with the first movement of Symphony No. 39; in so doing, we realize how they compliment each other in their opposition. Mozart returns to the symbol of duality and opposition in order to cap the work.

Starting from the initial chaos of the broken rhythms, the violence of the beats—in a word, from everything that the beginning of this triptych implies of darkness, anxiety, and disorder—Mozart leads us joyfully to light, rigor, and beauty: ritual terms in the Lodge. He has us glimpse, through the transparency of the first theme of Symphony No. 39, the clarity of hope. Then, in the darkness of Symphony No. 40, he has us struggle along the difficult initiatory path, made up of discouragements but also of moments of hope, in order to lead us to the foot of the Orient, faced with dazzling light, in the last symphony. As Mozart himself said a few weeks before in his letter to Puchberg, when he falls silent, he leaves us with his hope.

DIVERTIMENTO IN E FLAT MAJOR, "PUCHBERG TRIO" (K. 563)

Scarcely had Mozart finished the trilogy of symphonies in the first few days of August 1788 than he composed a song in favor of the Imperial Austrian war against the Turks, "in order to instruct and entertain the children during their free time," as the presentation text describes it. Mozart went to the trouble of entering in his catalog of works ten canons illustrating subjects ranging from the trivial to the crude. Were these works all composed in the course of the same summer? There is nothing to support that idea. What is interesting, however, is that soon after finishing the composition of the sublime Symphony No. 41, Wolfgang would take the time to return to his minor compositions and spend time on them. He seemed amused by these works with their superficial writing and lighthearted themes. As noted by the Massins, it is irrefutable that "at the time he is composing the symphonic trilogy, Mozart is closer to Rabelais than to Saint John of the Cross." Although none of these songs are worth studying, their presence at this particular moment in Mozart's life is interesting. The way in which he seems to have lived these two summer months allows each commentator to say what he likes and see what he wants to see.

Wolfgang hoped above all to leave behind the poverty that he always thought of as temporary. And to that end he approached his brothers and in particular Michael Puchberg, who from June to September 1788 seems more than ever to have been in evidence. Puchberg was the recipient of Wolfgang's letters of appeal, but also of compositions written in gratitude for his support. His letter of June 17, in which he addresses himself more to Puchberg as a brother than as a friend, ends with a significant postscript: "When are we going to make a little music once again at your place? I've written a new trio."

Conversations with Puchberg—except those in writing—were not only about money. As was the case with Puchberg, so it must have been between Mozart and other freemasons; we have seen this as well with the Divertimenti for wind instruments (K. 439b). Puchberg was not only someone with whom Mozart spoke about his material difficulties but also a friend in whom he found fraternal comfort and to whom he tended to express his gratitude. Mozart acted similarly in his gift of a concerto for clarinet offered to his brother Anton Stadler.

In a short span of time, from June to September, Puchberg received two trios for piano, one in E (K. 542) on June 22 and one in C (K. 548) on July 14. He received a third, the Trio in G (K. 564), on October 27.

The first of these trios, to which Mozart referred in his letter of June 17, confirmed his wish to find complete serenity in work.

Having completed the three last symphonies, Mozart returned to his brother Puchberg. But had he ever left him? Nor had he abandoned his Masonic beliefs; during the whole of the summer, they helped him rise above his distress. His worries explain and justify the composition of this new divertimento (K. 563)—a key work with respect to its symbolism. Indeed, why would Mozart have dedicated a new trio for strings to Puchberg after offering him two for piano in June and in July and was to offer him a third in October? The reason is that this diverimento arose from a very different and precise need. It was really a shared secret, or better still a work of collusion, complete with Masonic specificity, between Mozart and his benefactor brother. Would Puchberg understand and grasp this message? Mozart attached the most importance to this question.

If we dare say so, Mozart seemed to be nudging him in that direction. This composition does not have the rigorous form of the previous two trios. We have here a divertissement that actually includes six movements: an *allegro*, a minuet, an *andante*, another minuet with two trios, and a final *allegro*. What is notably exceptional in their character is that the first two movements embody an inspiration that is completely different from those that follow. They are not at all joyful or straightforward, which we might well have expected at the beginning of a work written for entertainment or the pleasure of listening.

It is likely that this trio was preceded by a first draft, the Trio in G (K. 562e), which was never finished; we might well wonder why it was not. It seems that it did not have sufficient weight and that the key of G major could appear, by its joyful coloring, too distant to express a Masonic thought. Once again, intentionally as a brother, Mozart repeated the meaningful key of E flat major with three points in the key signature. It's a brother who has helped me, he thought, and it's a brother whom I will thank by using fraternal language.

The first two movements are as if "constructed," since in fact they correspond to and complete each other. Hocquard writes, "We find in this prodigious work a recapitulation of the intellectual work found in the last two symphonies." Without giving justifications, the author implicitly recognizes—as he has done before—a similarity of writing and inspiration between the two symphonies and the divertimento. He is right in making this connection. However, the trio is not at all a recapitulation of the preceding works; it is completely autonomous. The similarity that Hocquard mentions is explained solely by the fact that the same spirit, Masonic ethics, underlies the composition of these works.

It is not surprising to find an identical process of writing in them; Mozart has recourse to the same symbols and uses them in the same way. The *allegro* is a movement of affirmation; the *adagio* is a movement of questioning—indicating a meaningful opposition using the symbol of contrasts. The melodic lines of the two movements' first bars are similar in design but reversed. In the first movement, a descent uses thirds with a coming together of the three instruments. In the second, on the contrary, a slow ascent again uses an arpeggio, also in thirds. We don't need to stress the symbolic value of using thirds, whose presence in this work is doubly evident.

The coming together of the melodic lines, and their reversal between the first two movements, bestows on the whole of the trio a much larger space. In the previous works, the process of writing that identified space was limited to the first movement only. In this trio, it is repeated in the second movement in order to confer a greater strength of conviction on the work.

The symbolism of space is equally evident in the third bar of the first movement. Between the scales of the violin on the one hand and those of the viola and cello on the other, the violin lightly expresses three "knocks." The vision of the musical writing becomes meaningful; these scales are like lines of escape toward a horizon where the three points are drawn.

The touching adagio of the second movement arises from an inspiration similar to what we have already seen in the processional Adagio (K. 411) or the Funeral Ode (K. 477). The expression of Mozart's Masonic thought is to be found throughout his life as an initiate, as well as in the works that this thinking inspired in him. We should not be surprised by this, since the content of the symbols, everlasting as they are, is the foundation of his inspiration. Putting them into music allows them to be perceived in the harmonies.

8

The Third Period: 1791

As was the case in 1788, the year 1791 was preceded by a period of profound discouragement. Mozart composed nothing during the second half of 1790. He traveled to Frankfurt at his own expense for the coronation of Leopold II, without having been invited, in the hope that he would be offered work composing or conducting. (However, he was still designated a musician of the Court.) Nothing came of the trip; it did not help him reestablish himself in the eyes of high society and was a financial disaster.

Under Leopold II, the Masonic order, as we have seen, had become suspect and was presumed to be dangerous to the authority of the State; in the eyes of the Austrian Court, the French Revolution was the result of the new ideas of the *Aufklärung* in Germany and freemasonry in Europe.

Mozart's adherence to freemasonry was known, but far from displaying a reserved attitude, which would perhaps help him return to grace, he portrayed great zeal in the public affirmation of his convictions. Here again we have proof that Mozart did not engage in double-dealing. While we have no convincing documents that would shed light on his attitude, we know that he faithfully attended the Lodges. Furthermore, it should be noted that his musical production toward the end of his life was largely devoted to celebrating his Masonic ideals. We can suppose that in the course of his trip to Frankfurt and neighboring cities, Mozart encountered freemasons coming from elsewhere in Europe for the coronation ceremonies who provided him with information about events in France. Whereas the revolution was unsettling for the Austrian authorities, it gave rise to rejoicing among those who, like Mozart, had already adopted its ideas.

It is very likely that the indifference and even disdain that greeted Mozart during the coronation ceremonies provoked in him a sharp reaction of opposition. He would been drawn closer to his only true friends, his brothers, with whom he shared the hope for the birth of a world that would be more just and fraternal: the world he had wanted to believe in ever since leaving Salzburg and entering the Masonic order.

Three concerns stood out in Mozart's correspondence to Constanze from Frankfurt. The first was his worries over his financial and material situation. In fact, before leaving, he had undertaken a loan burdened with complex guarantees; he continued to be concerned with the difficulties of getting it arranged. The second was his isolation, apparently intentional in order to avoid expenses, since he claimed nevertheless to have been acclaimed and admired: "I stay in for the whole morning, stuck with writing in my cubbyhole room." What was he writing? An adagio for mechanical organ that he "is only with difficulty able to bring to completion, so objectionable he finds the work." Seeing this blockage in his writing, we can imagine what helplessness and disgust Mozart must have felt when faced with the indifference of the high society that had gathered in Frankfurt. Did he have to keep writing for this fickle public? The mediocrity of commissions could hardly have enlivened his desire to write. So his third concern was to meet his real friends who, as he said himself, would help him. Among those he met, such as the flautist Johann Wendling, we especially notice Johann Boehm, the theatre director for whom he had reworked *Thamos* in Salzburg in 1779. All of them are freemasons. Thanks to them, he met the Frankfurt banker Franz Schweitzer and was welcomed by the Countess Hatzfeld, whom he had met in Vienna in 1781. Thanks to these last two, Mozart was able to give a concert in Frankfurt on October 15, his only success on the trip.

Shortly after his return from Frankfurt, Mozart entered a period of creativity. What are the reasons for this? He did not go immediately to Vienna. He stopped in Mayence where he played at the home of the Prince Elector* for a pitiful sum, then he traveled on to Mannheim where he stayed longer than expected, giving advice to the theatrical troupe that was putting on *The Marriage of Figaro*. On each of his visits there, Mannheim continued to be the city where he was happy. He even wrote to Constanze that he wanted to come back to Mannheim with her the following year. He performed once again for the Prince Elector, thus gaining confidence with each of these contacts during his homeward journey: "Excuse me if I don't write you as often as I would like; but you cannot imagine how people run after me," he said in a letter to his wife from Munich on November 2, 1790.

The sterile year of 1790 ended, making way for a year of

---

*[A prince of the Holy Roman Empire entitled to elect the Emperor. —*Trans.*]

intense creativity, which can be explained only by a renewed self-confidence. During the period from December 1790 to December 1791, the count is thirty-eight works, certainly of varying importance: among them, two operas, two quintets, a concerto, three cantatas, arias, dances, and the beginning of the Requiem.

Upon his return to Vienna, Mozart was again faced with the same material difficulties he had experienced before his departure for Frankfurt—in fact, the same difficulties as in 1788. It is amazing to realize that this similarity in despair would give birth to works of similar inspiration. We know that the suffering he went through in 1788 gave rise to, among other works, the creation of the last three symphonies. At the end of 1790, Mozart reacted in an identical way; his inspiration would draw once again on his Masonic beliefs.

As with the previous periods, we will not examine the works from the List except for the last two quintets, the D major (K. 593) and the E flat major (K. 614), as well as the Concerto for Clarinet (K. 622). As for *The Magic Flute*, a work that has already been so analyzed and dissected, we will mention only the importance and the role of the symbols, since this opera brings out both illustrative music for the description of the initiation and inspirational music for the symbolism. This dual nature, never having been analyzed deductively or without prejudice, has given rise to errors in appreciation.

QUINTET FOR STRINGS IN D MAJOR (K. 593)

This quintet from December 1790 begins the last twelve months of Mozart's life. After the previous almost sterile period, it takes on a wholly individual meaning, forming a turning point between regaining his self-confidence and the intense creativity that precedes his death.

Like the following quintet (K. 614, written in April 1791), this work was commissioned by Johann Tost, a freemason and Hungarian amateur violinist. We can assume that this commission was a fraternal gesture since Tost was aware of Mozart's hardships. The remuneration he received must have been important. Tost was a wealthy and generous businessman who had already commissioned quartets from Haydn. Because it was written in the same spirit of fraternity, it is of a similar nature to the trio dedicated to Puchberg (K. 563). In both cases, we have compositions dedicated to brothers, requiring a specific language that can be understood by both giver and receiver.

We spoke earlier of collusion with Puchberg, and we need to mention it again with Tost. Were they able to appreciate the total value of the symbolic writing in these works into which Mozart had put so much of himself? That they didn't understand the richness of his thought or the intensity of his conviction matters little. Mozart did not write these works solely in order that his two brothers would have the privilege and joy of discovering in them symbols that were clear only to initiates. The "Puchberg Trio" and the quintets for Tost are in fact not illustrative works. Mozart spoke to his brothers out of respect for them as he must, with discretion but also with conviction, knowing that through them he would forever confide to humanity his vision of beauty and serenity.

Appropriately, the symbols with which we are acquainted are present in this work from the first bars. The initial movement is preceded by a *larghetto* in B minor, in which an arpeggio using an ascending third, expressed gravely by the cello, forms the first bar. It is most natural to connect the expression of this arpeggio, a veritable question, with that already encountered in the first measures of the Adagio for piano in B minor (K. 540), written in March 1788. To this question from the cello, all the instruments respond with a surprising tenderness. This dialogue is built up in six repetitions and seems to express the anguish before an initiatory voyage. We are dealing with a moment of anxiety and concern.

Such a procedure is extremely rare in chamber music. We encountered it only in 1785 with the "Dissonance" Quartet (K. 465). The specificity there is to be found identically in this quintet in D. An important element further confirms its Masonic specificity: it is the basic similarity of this introductory *larghetto* to that of the Masonic adagio for wind instruments (K. 411). We have confirmation that Mozart employed the same language that he did in the significant period of 1785 and the painful period of 1788.

The first movement is engraved with this spirit of will, determination, and self-mastery, a symbol differing only in the smaller scope of its writing from that which characterizes Symphony No. 40 in G minor.

This *allegro* displays another meaningful characteristic of the works inspired by symbolism. It consists of the break in the movement, musically inexplicable, arising from the unexpected insertion of a theme that is different in nature and rhythm from the main one. This procedure of a break also characterized the second movement of Concerto No. 20 in D minor (K. 466), as well as the last two movements of Concerto No. 22 in E flat major (K. 482). In this quintet, the effect of a break is obtained before the last bars of the first movement by reintroducing identically the initial arpeggio in B minor from the introductory *larghetto*.

For a great many musicologists, the second movement constitutes a high point of all music. It displays the same characteristics of inspiration and writing as those that mark the second movements of his inspired works, the function of which is to respond to the query posed by the first movement. Here again, anxiety and anguish are vanquished by serenity and light in the music. We find again in this second movement, adagio, a comparable expression and thought, expressed in a similar form of composition, to that of the *andante* of Symphony No. 41. According to what he wants to express, Mozart is inspired by different symbols, always present in the composition as vectors of his thought. Saint-Foix sees in this quintet "the intensification of human suffering while at the same time the detachment from all exterior things: all this clearly shows Mozart's humble acceptance and a resignation that is entirely Christian." We might well be astonished by such an opinion. What "resignation" can there be in a work that on the contrary launches a period of affirmation and exceptional creativity in reaction to a period of sterile silence? Mozart accepted nothing of what had wounded him in Frankfurt. We see no hint of resignation, Christian or otherwise, in this quintet written from the sole impulse of his Masonic beliefs.

QUINTET FOR STRINGS IN E FLAT MAJOR (K. 614)

This quintet is the last that Mozart wrote. It dates from April 12, 1791. The despair of the preceding months had been conquered. We have seen with the winter compositions how, his confidence renewed, Mozart was able to overcome his anguish. His spiritual strength was drawn in large measure on his Masonic ideal and remained comforted by the encouragement of his brothers, whose presence since the fall had proved most valuable. Like the previous quintet in D major, this one is dedicated to his brother Tost. It is therefore not surprising that it is inspired by the same ideal and is therefore the same writing. However, unlike the previous quintet, this one expresses no anxiety but only limpidity and calm. All the musical impulses in previous pieces that show inner tension are superseded. Belgian musicologist Harry Halbreich sees in the *andante* of this quartet "the expression of an undeniable power of emotion within a cheery clarity." Continuing, he says that it is "the quintessence of the later Mozart for whom the second serenity is nothing less than the dearly won result of the conquering of the most dreadful despair and is to be found well beyond all passion."

The work is written in E flat major; the deliberate use of the symbol of the three signature points again appears clearly. Once more we see the complicity that Mozart wants to share with his brother Tost, just as he had shared it with Puchberg three years before. But there is more; Mozart intentionally expresses this key by a structure, arpeggiated in thirds, as he has done many times before (most distinctly for the theme of the first movement of Symphony No. 39).

If the use of the ternary symbol for the key is fundamental in a work inspired by freemasonry, we can see that, within the whole of Mozart's creation, the key of E flat major (and its related key, C minor) had acquired an undeniable significance. Mozart returned to this key with its symbolic character because he knew that its creative power had become what he would use from this point on to express serenity.

It is interesting that all commentators have noticed the essentially calming character of this quintet. Without being aware of it, they use the same vocabulary that we use to justify its Masonic character. We cannot say it better than they do; we need only borrow a few of their remarks: "Work which is devoid of tears, where there is no thought of darkness, of suffering" (Henri Ghéon); "the last quintet concludes the chamber music with a luminous distillation of its sound fabric; it prolongs the ascent into impalpable light" (Hocquard); "song from the heart that breathes beyond the visible world" (Adolf Boschot); "its spiritual abundance is in inverse proportion to its material poverty" (Girdlestone); "it is relatively easy to notice everything that unites or brings this quintet closer to mystical elements, elements beyond time, those that run through *The Magic Flute*. This quintet expresses the state of its creator's soul, now delivered from all passionate obsessions and therefore more likely than ever to soar toward regions where there reigns the serene enthusiasm of beings freed from attachment to the world" (Saint-Foix).

Musicologists are unanimous in recognizing in this quintet the perfect transcription of inspiration through symbols, an inspiration present but hidden from December 1784 onward. "Ascent into light," "beyond the visible world," "spiritual abundance," "mystical elements," the soul "delivered from all passionate obsessions": these words are the same as those we have found throughout this book to demonstrate the Masonic influence in Mozart's work and to recognize it as a permanent source of his inspiration.

CONCERTO FOR CLARINET IN A MAJOR (K. 622)

This concerto, dated October 7, 1791, is Mozart's last concerto. Its place among Mozart's works deserves special attention. In fact, if we make an exception for the opera *The Clemency of Titus* (K. 621), a commissioned work not directly related to Mozart's personal creative concerns during the summer of 1791, it falls within the most intense and overtly Masonic production time of all. It is preceded by the Little German Cantata (K. 619) and *The Magic Flute*, a Masonic opera (K. 620), and followed by the grand Masonic Cantata (K. 623) and the Masonic Song (K. 623a). It needs to be recognized that, in these last three months, Mozart's creative concerns were wholly those of an initiate who was more ardent by the day.

During this time he wrote to Constanze, who was staying at Baden, that he "finishes the rondo for Stadler (actually, the concerto for clarinet), while smoking a wonderful pipe." During this painful summer he thought about his old freemason friend Anton Stadler, an excellent clarinetist, who had commissioned the composition of a concerto. At a time when he had other works to finish (including the Requiem), nothing was pushing Mozart to devote his genius to a composition that was not really all that urgent. Moreover, we know that Stadler owed Mozart money, so it wasn't for financial reasons that he sought to satisfy his friend. One financial reason that was truly constraining and ought to have pushed him to compose: he had not delivered to Count Franz Walsegg-Stuppach the Requiem for which he had received an advance several months before. He was doing nothing about it.

We know that Mozart continued to attend Lodge assemblies. On November 18, a few days before his death, he was among his brothers, to whom he offered his last work written on the occasion of the outfitting of a new temple. The expression of his Masonic convictions entirely occupied the remainder of his life and shone forth more strongly than ever in the compositions of this period.

Receiving more applause every evening, *The Magic Flute* openly glorified this expression. For those initiated, the Concerto for Clarinet expresses the same thing no less clearly but with the required discretion.

This concerto, as far as we know, was the result of Mozart's previous investigations that had given rise to sketches but also to the great Quintet for Clarinet (K. 581), composed for his brother Stadler and dated September 28, 1789. That quintet was itself preceded by the Adagio for English horn, two horns, and bassoon (K. 580a), which, as we have mentioned, was written for Masonic ceremonies and provided the theme for the *Ave Verum*. The inspiration that characterizes this adagio appears once again in the quintet for clarinet.

The preparation for the composition of the concerto itself is exceedingly complex. The work was preceded by a broad sketch of a concerto for basset horn in G major, also written for Stadler. (This musician excelled as much in this instrument as in the clarinet.) The two hundred-odd bars that have come down to us correspond fairly closely to the first half of the concerto for clarinet.

A fraternal and Masonic atmosphere surrounds this concerto's creation. It is reflected in the piece's musical expression: a character of intensity, calm, and warmth. The quintet and the concerto, whose writing and inspiration are marked with the same influence, both arise from the same Masonic vision. Harmony and belief come together in them. Everything is inspired and constructed according to a perfect balance, as much in the lyricism of the quintet as in the majesty of the concerto. This poetry is expressed once again by the clarinet, which over the years had become for Mozart the confidant of his secret. All virtuosity, all exuberance are banished from these works, while the movements that follow a faster rhythm in no way express elation but only simple happiness.

In October 1791, Mozart had only two months to live. Did he know that he would not be given more time? It is impossible to reply with certainty. However, we can see that, although the idea of death concerned him during these two months, he did not fear it and his work showed no evidence of it. From this point on, he tried to reinforce his beliefs and think of death in the way he had described it in 1787: as the best friend of man. In the course of his last weeks, the works that he strove to complete express through their total serenity the inescapable march toward the eternal Orient.

In order to be more precise, it is appropriate to add that in September Mozart composed an aria for bass, "Io ti lascio" ("I Leave Thee," K. 621a), and he did so a few moments before leaving Prague where *The Clemency of Titus* had just been performed. He sensed that he was never to return. This very short aria in which Mozart expressed an intense emotion was in reality the painful but thoughtful farewell to this city where he had lived with fame and happiness and where, above all, he had always been welcomed with fraternity. Although some consider this aria a farewell to love and life, for us it is certainly a farewell to friendship and fraternity.

THE MAGIC FLUTE (K. 620)

In the case of *The Magic Flute*, the reader has available a vast number of works written over the course of almost two centuries by authors whose interpretations continue to diverge. The complexity of this opera is such that each person can see in it what he likes.

Remy Stricker writes that "the more we read commentaries, the more our ideas vacillate." Jacques Chailley's opinion is that "the spectator who goes to a performance of this opera has to be puzzled: the first act begins with a fairy tale and the second is even more incomprehensible."

Mozart's last opera, written a few months before his death, clearly confirms the permanence and solidity of his attachment to his Masonic ideals right up to the end of his life. Contrary to what its appearance could lead one to think, it is not at all a piece of fantasy. Besides, it is significant that from its first performance the public understood and appreciated its true, profound meaning. In letters to Constanze, Mozart expressed his joy in realizing "how this opera continues to rise in importance in the eyes of the public; what I appreciate most is the success conveyed by silence"—a silence, however, that was rarely present during performances. Mozart was very sensitive to the attitude of his public, which listened and reflected before applauding; he was also sensitive to Salieri's perfect understanding of the libretto. Goethe, also a freemason, perceived perfectly the profound meaning of the work and the value of its message. He considered *The Magic Flute* to be one of the most beautiful and most noble of operas; he even began writing a sequel to it.

Mozart expressed his joy at having been initiated, but more importantly confirmed that his beliefs had not weakened since 1784. *The Magic Flute* turns out to be a veritable declaration of faith, which Mozart very deliberately expressed publicly, regardless of the risks involved at a time when the Order was beginning to be persecuted.

What were the underlying reasons that impelled Mozart to overtly compose a controversial work? It would be plausible that Mozart and his librettist and fellow freemason Emanuel Schikaneder composed *The Magic Flute* in order to present free-masonry in a favorable light, less to glorify than defend it. They might have wanted to show that the Order was not a dangerous or suspect political organization, but only an initiatory and fraternal organization. In this case, Mozart would have been composing less out of bravado than a desire to defend the respectable object of his convictions. Whatever his real reason might be, this composition is a deliberate and calculated act, in which his genius proclaims his beliefs.

Nor does it seem that Mozart accepted the offer from his brother for financial reasons, even though in the spring of 1791 any amount of money coming in must have been welcome. Indeed, contrary to the opinion disseminated by his first biographers, we know today that Mozart did not propose the subject of the play to Schikaneder; rather it was Schikaneder who, knowing Wolfgang's difficult circumstances, proposed the creation of this work with the obvious aim of helping him in a brotherly way.

Enthusiastically, Wolfgang then agreed to mount a German opera. For his theatrical performances, Schikaneder already had available an important repertoire of this kind of play *(singspiel)*. Mozart was convinced right away. In fact he knew that *singspiel* were appreciated more and more every day, and not only in Vienna. He had learned that his first *singspiel*, *The Abduction from the Seraglio*, was enjoying a new and immense success across the Germanic world. What a windfall for Wolfgang to be able to put on once again an opera of the kind he had always loved and which he had even defended against Italian opera a few years before! Without any doubt, he also remembered *Thamos*, whose subject matter was very similar to what Schikaneder was proposing to him now—this *Thamos* that, on two occasions, had been the object of his attentive care.

This time, Wolfgang worked on the libretto himself, and he therefore shaped his own conception of the subject matter and its unfolding. From his earlier correspondence, we know that Mozart brought an individual and rigorous attention to the construction of the plots of his operas (especially *The Magic Flute*), and to the words, which, for him, needed to be molded to the music. With this opera, Mozart no longer depended on anyone. The libretto was not imposed on him but only proposed. He did not have to battle some music director to obtain the modifications that he wished to bring to his work.

The freemason Johann Georg Metzler (Giesecke) and the Grand Master Ignaz von Born—the model for Sarastro—likely also participated in the development of the libretto. Schikaneder, however, remained the principal author or, more accurately, principal adaptor. Actually, he was directly and broadly inspired by similar fashionable works performed at this period on the Vienna stage. Mozart's participation in the libretto is essential and indisputable. Knowing his character, we can be certain that, if he had had any misgivings, he would not have devoted a second of his time to it. A work that is so refined musically can only have been elaborated with complete agreement between the two brothers, regarding the subject matter as much as the conception of the staging. Their close collaboration and their being of the same mind are especially evident in the harmonious selection of texts to be spoken as opposed to those chosen to become arias. Without this concern for a unity of vision in the foundation, the spirit, and the unfolding of the play, it all could have led to a disparate work deprived of the slightest interest. On the contrary, the diversity of musical themes, adapted to multiple situations in the scenario, is like a variety of colors illuminating the subject matter.

With *The Magic Flute,* are we dealing with a Masonic composition that narrates the ritual of a ceremony, or rather a work that is inspired by symbolism in the way we have been using that term? The opera as a whole intentionally shows the effects of Masonic spirit but, no less intentionally, waters down the ritual and weakens the content of the symbols. This is what we have already felt in the analysis of *Thamos,* but in that case the effect was less significant since *Thamos* takes nothing from the ceremony of an assembly or an initiation, as is done in *The Magic Flute.*

We in the audience are not in the Lodge and cannot imagine being there; the absence of the initiate excludes any possibility of a descent of the sacred; the ceremony of the ritual is therefore divorced from its power. *The Magic Flute* then relates and partially reproduces the ceremony of initiation without betraying its spirit. The Masonic character, for example, is confirmed by the presence of three children who represent the three officers who must be present at a request for admission to the Order. Mozart's heartfelt convictions and fond memories imbue the work with emotion, since there is no spectators' participation to allow the bringing of the sacred to the work.

The work in its totality is no more circumstantial than that. Except for the overture and the march of the priests, which are precisely not overt, no aria from the opera could be performed in the Lodge as an accompaniment to a moment in the Masonic liturgy.

Some commentators have thought that, in his opera, Mozart betrayed the secrets of freemasonry by divulging them to a secular public. Such a conclusion is inaccurate. Masonic liturgy is readily available in bookstores, having been widely published. Besides, the initiation ceremony is only partially included in the opera; it is intentionally depicted in only a limited way. The text of the libretto does not reflect the terms of the liturgy. On the contrary, the descriptive elements that Mozart retained—although in the context of an opera they cannot be bearers of the sacred—are the most representative and spectacular in the ceremony, quite suitable for staging.

Since it is not ritual but narrative, *The Magic Flute* cannot be thought of as expressing the esoteric content of symbols, as is the case of the last symphonies, for example. Citing Masonic themes makes the work completely overt. A number of the symbols that we have studied appear in the opera but they are present for their narrative value only. However, in being expressed accurately and honestly, they confer their Masonic meaning on it.

Two scenes recall Mozart's memory of his initiation. When Tamino tries to move into the temple, he is at first brutally rejected, then in the end welcomed by the priest. The two engage in a dialogue (an exchange of a surprising emotional intensity) that, violent at first, becomes calm. Mozart brings to this moment the actual feelings of fear of the layman knocking at the door of the temple, fears that he himself has lived through.

The second scene is the chorale of the two armed men welcoming Tamino and Pamina before the trial by water and fire. This chorale brings to life for the spectator the impression of fear experienced by Mozart, as with any postulant, in the face of the trials imposed by the ritual. By connecting these two scenes with the recitative of the priest in *Thamos*, we become aware of just what the initiation gave Mozart. The moving and profound words of *The Magic Flute* really bear fear and hope, since they are those of an initiate expressing what he has undergone. This was not the case at the time *Thamos* was composed.

Although the main theme of the opera is the quest for wisdom and serenity, this is not its only one. If *The Magic Flute* were only an homage to freemasonry or a defense of it, it would not have held the public's favor through the centuries just as it did for the first spectators in the autumn of 1791. It is a work that, through initiation, sings of the attainment of happiness and felicity through love. It is in this aspect that the opera differs profoundly from the previous ones of a secular character in which love, intense though it may be, does not really bring to one's heart the harmony of a perfect happiness. Even the toast from the second act of *Così Fan Tutte*, although it is one of the most moving expressions of happiness, is dramatized by trickery and lies. Of Mozart's operas, only *The Magic Flute* expresses serenity in the light and clarity of truth.

At least at the beginning, the opera's characters are not considered real human beings; they appear more as fairy tale figures outside reality. They are entities bringing myth and image, which explains the lack of a real plot woven around creatures of flesh. If there is a plot, it is built up not from situations but rather from questions: Can good vanquish evil? Can any layman be initiated? Beyond the originality of what is scarcely a plot, the main driving force of the action turns out to be the following: in spite of the diversity of their culture, their beliefs, or their social standing, all men have the right to attain happiness and love. For such a subject one must have a morality similar to that referred to throughout the libretto: the man who takes as an ideal the attainment of the light reaches through initiation to a greater, purer happiness and a more perfect love. This is the way Mozart solves the issue posed between the beginning and the end of the work—an issue that is too often presented as incoherent. The protagonists belong to the world of imagination in the first scenes; later they become human beings. The symbolism of the initiation and its representation on the stage blends into the light and gives way to moments of humanity.

The overture and the march of the priests at the beginning of the second act are the only moments in the opera that are not overt. These two movements resort to symbolism: the first in its inspiration, the second in its ritual structure.

The overture has continued to give rise to debates that entail taking positions that are as fixed as they are contradictory. Only with reference to the symbolism and a ritual that has been actually experienced in the Lodge can there be a simple and accurate analysis of this overture. Too many assumptions and preconceived interpretations have guided commentators in their research. A subject that has to do with fairy-like esotericism is likely to turn one's thoughts to mystery, but such an approach does nothing to further the understanding of the true inspiration behind the overture; in fact it does the opposite. In this overture, as in the rest of the opera, Masonic references are precise but actually few and far between. Mozart limited himself to a few symbols and above all to simple ones. He did not play with them, as if to render them even more hermetic. The reference to them is clear and they are completely specific to freemasonry even though they may not be noticed by the layman.

In particular, it is totally inaccurate to see in the overture any reference whatever to the third degree, a reference that would be justified by the beats of three times three "knocks" appearing at the beginning of the second part of the overture. Three "knocks" repeated three times continuously can indeed constitute the drumming of the third degree. But if the three beats are separated by a

The Magic Flute, *overtures for the first and second parts*

moment of silence (for example, when they are struck successively by three different people, as is done by the Master and the two Wardens), then it is a matter of the simple beats that relate to the opening of the Lodge referring to the first degree.

We have already seen in *Thamos* the lack of a message when the chords are not ritual. This is why the other famous five chords that are found at the beginning of the overture to *The Magic Flute* are nothing more, from a symbolic point of view, than the expression of intentional mistakes (see the score for the two overtures). Mozart means by this deliberate mistake that the first moments of the opera leave the spectator in the secular world, precisely the world of mistakes and errors. If these five chords, following the interpretation of Jacques Chailley, stand for feminine beats, we might ask by what Masonic justification they are said to precede those of the masculine beats. Such a sequence in no way arises from a symbolic or ritual constraint. In addition, the two sets of beats, the first of five and the second of nine, if we were to accept the meaning that Jacques Chailley assigns them, could portray two initiations of different characters, one masculine, the other feminine. But initiation has no gender. The two heroes are initiated together during the same ceremony. The first five beats signify only the secular world of error; they are quite naturally opposed to the three times three beats stated at the beginning of the second part and by means of which we make our way into the world of initiates.

Composed of two deliberately distinct parts both in their nature and in their writing, the overture sets forth in advance the different staging content of the two acts: the first describes, using an uncoordinated rhythm and melodic line, the secular, uncrafted world; the second, beginning with nine ritual beats, means that we have left this secular world; in order to present an image, Mozart crafts a melodic line that has the rigor of a fugue.

With this overture, Mozart tells us unambiguously that the opera in its totality is situated and remains at the first degree, that of Entered Apprentice. This is the degree to which the neophyte is initiated and in the course of which he receives the light. The opera offers no other meanings and deals only with the one initiation. It is useless to look for symbols of a higher Masonic degree. We cannot share the view of Autexier, who believes that the initiation we are witnessing is the second degree.[1] The second degree, that of Fellowcraft, makes no reference to the four elements that accompany the trials or the approach of the light. The symbol of the second degree is essentially that of man in his relations with himself, the external world, and the cosmos. Autexier goes further: "Mozart and Schikaneder could not, in a single play, represent distinctly the three usual degrees." In fact, they never considered representing them, or attempted to. After the scenes of happiness that precede the end of the opera, a happiness that Tamino and Pamina reach through their initiation only to the first degree, how could the authors logically have been able to include the representation of the dramatic scene of the murder of Hiram and the mystical rebirth that follows? How would they have been able to invoke, in an atmosphere of rejoicing, a symbol of death? Mozart's opera contains enough symbols that clearly carry a message. Why uselessly imagine higher degrees that are more mysteriously hidden than ever?

The march of the priests is not inspired by a particular symbol, but covertly, this scene presents all the characteristics we have already encountered in the Masonic works for special occasions. This march in itself could belong to the famous List. In the majesty of its theme and its processional rhythm, it is akin to the adagio from Symphony No. 26 (K. 184), the Adagio for English horn, two horns, and bassoon (K. 580a), and the Adagio for wind instruments (K. 411). We understand that certain Lodges wishing to retain its deeper meaning perform this march even today in the course of their ceremonies.

We have said that only the presence of the number three at the head of the score has a Masonic value, and the presence of flats has no such value. Here, the specificity of keys with flats is of a harmonic nature, not a symbolic one. It seems necessary to return to this topic concerning certain analyses that have been made and most particularly that of Chailley, since his work makes an important study of it. To recall what he says: "From the mix of this symphony (that of flats) with that of Number is born the hieratic preeminence of E flat major, which reunites at one and the same time the number three for perfection, the major mode for serenity and the flats for weight." That a key in flats (not only E flat) might present to the ear more smoothness or emotional power seems to be demonstrated by experience. Musicians know how to take advantage of this specificity, which arises from harmony but is not at all symbolic. The major mode is perhaps more serene than the minor (although that remains to be proven) but has no connection to symbolism. Only the number three implies a specific symbolism—that of perfection.

We cannot follow Chailley further when he goes on to claim that the protagonists, who in the course of the opera speak in keys with flats, are worthy of initiation while those who have available to them only keys with sharps cannot be worthy. There is no reference to the world of Masonic symbolism that would support such an opinion or such an interpretation. What is correct (but has nothing to do with symbolism) is what Chailley adds without noticing the contradiction among his different assertions: "Tamino, Pamina, Sarastro, Papageno, The Queen of the Night all have their musical color, which follows them throughout the course of the action." This musical color, unique for each character, results in fact from the choice of a key that identifies each one, and has nothing to do with whether that character is worthy of initiation or not. Such connections are based on harmony and sound; they have nothing to do with any symbolism whatever, certainly not Masonic symbolism.

With *The Magic Flute*, a hymn of recognition to the grandeur of the Order, Mozart did not abandon the theme of love, which was always the real inspiration for his operas. This feeling is triumphant in the work, as much for those who undergo their initiation as for those who remain laymen. It's not without reason that the union of Papageno and Papagena, both joyful and profane, comes after the initiation scene, contrary to what Ingmar Bergman thought was better in his film. The director was trying to have light and wisdom triumph and through this reversal he conferred a more intense emotion on the theme of initiation. This reversal in the staging of the film makes the end of the opera more dramatic and accords it a Masonic priority. Mozart and Schikaneder did not want it that way.

Mozart repeatedly refered to human emotions and sang praises to their beauty. His intention is clear with regard to Pamino and Papageno in the first act. They both express an identical vision of love. Later, each one separately wants to commit suicide and the three children halt their identical gestures of despair. Although the opera destines Pamina to Tamino, Mozart nonetheless has her approach Papageno in a marvelous duo in the first act. This duo celebrates human love as a hymn with a profound and simple tenderness, expressed to perfection by the balance in the song. Although it does not really bear a symbol, this aria in E flat major uses thirds to express by its clarity the aspiration to happiness, a happiness almost as perfect as that given by the initiation.

At the end of the opera, the meeting of Papageno and Papagena, filled with an entirely secular joy, remains for Mozart just as necessary and as full of meaning as that which took place earlier between the two initiates. Through the tenderness, the gaiety, and the purity of the music, Mozart ascribes to this meeting a value that may be different, but is very close to that of initiation. The bars that sing of this encounter, although they are not right at the end, in fact conclude the opera. We cannot accept the victory of Sarastro over the world of the Queen of the Night as the real conclusion of *The Magic Flute*, just as it is impossible to take the chorale of elation that follows the damnation of Don Juan as the real conclusion of that opera. In both cases, we are dealing with a conventional closure without artistic or psychological meaning (what might be called today a "happy ending").

The finale of *The Magic Flute* sings not only about the Royal Art and the perfection and wisdom to which initiation can lead, but just as much about the triumph and purity of feelings and of the heart.

9

Wolfgang's Legacy

Perhaps it is necessary to return to the debate, useless in my eyes, but still alive today: Was Mozart's last work the Requiem or the Masonic cantata (K. 623)? Still today, each person, referring only to his own convictions, tends to opt for one or other of these works. It's immensely misguided to substitute personal opinion for fact. Such a view does not take into account undeniable, chronological facts or, above all, the concerns that Mozart considered fundamental during the first half of November 1791.

This view has an even more serious flaw watering down the debate; it contrasts two ideologies, the Christian and the Masonic, in a valuation of them that is simplified and contemporary, therefore anachronistic. It cannot be stated too strongly that for the freemasons of the eighteenth century, these two sets of beliefs were perfectly reconcilable. Initiation does not make a believer into a condemned atheist. By writing a mass or a Masonic cantata, Mozart presents an identical vision of his conception of divinity. Let us not forget that the *Ave Verum*, which was for Olivier

Messiaen the most religious music there ever was, uses the musical line from the Masonic Adagio for English horn (K. 580a), a borrowing that is conceivable because Mozart's vision of the divine is identical in both works.

Commentators seem not to take into account musicological data that is fundamental in explaining the unity of Wolfgang's beliefs; on the contrary, they seek to oppose it. This bias explains that, for some people, "the Requiem is not only a religious work but a Catholic one."[1] How can one go so far, and how could music called Catholic be superior to other music? Following such a line of thought, the Mass in C minor (K. 427) by the Catholic Mozart (although never finished) must be superior to the Mass in B minor by the Protestant J. S. Bach. We are astonished to read in the same article: "[F]or the first time in his life, Mozart (in the Requiem) is looking above himself in music, he sees no one and holds forth. This mass for the dead, which Mozart never took the trouble to finish, seems to have been the only work that was 'too much for him.'"[2] This nearly relentless desire to have Mozart die within the Catholic Church negates any serious value in an analysis of the matter. In reality, Mozart's great works that are inspired by symbols reflect the same vision of what stands above human nature. They belong to the world of hope and serenity, not to any particular religion. So Mozart has no need to "hold forth"; his work was never a cry but rather a continual revelation. Love, light, and death are one in his music, to such a degree that a single theme sometimes contains all three.

In order to consider Mozart's work with tolerance, there is no advantage in insisting that the Masonic cantata (K. 623) of November 15, 1791, was chronologically the last of Mozart's works, one in which he would try to express his last wishes. Here we have another error of judgment with regard to this question: Does the Requiem or the cantata constitute Wolfgang's legacy? If today we can ask this question (however useless it might be), it could never have been asked of Mozart. On November 15, even though worried and suffering, he could not have known that he was to die within three weeks, especially since he attended a Lodge assembly in good health three days later. This is why neither the Requiem nor the cantata has the value of a legacy. Any analysis that attempts to consider them as such is prejudiced since it is unrealistic. Mozart did not finish the Requiem commissioned six months before because he didn't feel the need to do so, and the "formula" of the mass did not suit him (or, more accurately, did not suit him in the autumn of 1791). His vision of the Beyond and death had no need to be expressed in the structure of a pre-established and confining religious text. If we refer to the parts of the Requiem that Mozart finished, we see that he rejects nothing of the text or its spirit. On the contrary, certain words and phrases carry an exceptional and meaningful orchestration. However, it is not the content of the religious text that constitutes the inspiration itself. Only the vision of the Beyond remains for Mozart, during these last moments of his life, the direct source of his inspiration. From his letter of April 4, 1787, we know his vision of death. This death before a "god of judgment" participates in divinity, but it in no way implies an act of submission or contrition.

In Mozart's works, the painful expression of death is always accompanied by the radiant clarity that transfigures it. In such a light was the Funeral Ode of 1785 already concluded.

It would not be surprising that the Requiem, which stopped with the "Lacrymosa," continues into the cantata, which finishes in the light. Far from being opposed, these two works are in reality one in Mozart's mind in 1791.

Feeling responsible to Count Walsegg, who commissioned the work, Mozart would certainly have finished this mass for the dead, but he saw no reason at that particular moment to apply himself once again to his inspiration and the composition of a commissioned work that would in any case remain anonymous. Neither any impending idea of his own death, nor anxiety motivated by the composition of a funeral mass, troubled Mozart. Rather, he was annoyed at having to work once again at the end of autumn on a confining liturgical text while all his works since July that were not commissioned proclaimed the attainment of serenity through joy and love.

In fact, saying that Mozart lacked the time to finish the Requiem commissioned five months before would be equivalent to refusing to understand either his character or his creative powers. Such an argument has no value. We should recall that he needed less than two months to create his last three symphonies. Moreover, the amount of composition missing from the Requiem is approximately equal to the duration of the Masonic cantata. Why then was the amount of time spent on the cantata not devoted to the Requiem? For the reason that we have already put forward: an identical inspiration underlies both works. They were conceived and created in the same period of time, and were based on an inspiration that reflects an identical vision of the blessed state beyond death.

The light of the "divine Mozart" is the way Adolphe Boschot and Roland Barthes speak of Wolfgang: a way that no one has ever found pretentious or excessive. Conscious of the universal and eternal meaning of the symbols acquired through his initiation, Mozart leads man in harmony beyond simple earthly existence. An astonishing perception of serenity, love, and light: his music reveals that these qualities are divinity for him.

Mozart apprehends the human being, his feelings, his pain, and his hope; then, effacing himself in the expression of the purest harmony, just as the symbol effaces itself in its eternal content, he leaves man alone in the light, facing the revelation of his own reason for being.

Appendix 1

Works Officially Recognized as Masonic

Marches

K. 410: Adagio, 2 basset horns, 1 bassoon (1785)

K. 411: Adagio, 2 clarinets, 3 basset horns (1785)

K. 477: Masonic Funeral March, orchestra (1785)

Songs

K. 53: An die Freude ["To Joy"] (1768)

K. 125f: Die Zufriedenheit im niedrigen Stande ["Satisfaction in Low Places"] (1772);

K. 148: O heiliges Band der Freundschaft ["O Hallowed Bond of Friendship"] (1772)

K. 468: Die Gesellenreise ["The Fellowcraft's Journey"] (1785)

Cantatas

K. 429: Dir, Seele des Weltalls ["To Thee, Soul of the Universe"] (1785)

K. 471: Die Maurerfreude ["The Mason's Joy"] (1785)

K. 483: Zerfliesset heut' ["Today Be Moved, Dear Brothers"] (1785)

K. 484: Ihr, unsre neuen Leiter ["To You, Our Leaders New"] (1785)

K. 619: Die ihr des unermesslichen Weltalls ["You Who Revere the Creator of the Boundless Universe," the Little German Cantata] (1791)

K. 623: Laut verkünde unsre Freude ["Loudly Proclaim Our Joy," the Grand Masonic Cantata] (1791)

K. 623a: Lasst uns mit Geschlungen Händen ["Let Us Join Our Hands," the Masonic Song] (1791)

Operas

K. 345: *Thamos, König in Ägypten [Thamos, King of Egypt]* (1773 and 1779)

K. 620: *Die Zauberflöte [The Magic Flute]* (1791)

Appendix 2

Mozart's Attendance in the Lodges of Vienna

Notes extracted from *Mozart, les Documents de sa Vie Rassemblés et Expliqués par von Otto Erich Deutch* (Kassel: Barenreiter, 1961).

5
57 _____ 84*
XII

Communiqué from the Lodge "zur Wohltätigkeit" ("Charity") to sister Lodges in Vienna:

Proposal concerning the choirmaster, Wolfgang Amadeus Mozart. "Our former secretary Hoffmann neglected to inform the sister Lodges of this proposal. Notification of it had been given more than four weeks before to the District Lodge. We wish, further to this fact, to proceed to his initiation (that of Mozart) unless the sister Lodges have any objection they wish to raise.

SIGNED: SECRETARY . . . SCHWANCKHARDT."

---

*Ritual representation of December 5, 1784 (5784 being the year of "true light")

14

57 _____ 84

XII

[December 14, 5784/AD 1784]

Communiqué from the Lodge "Charity" to sister Lodges in Vienna:

On 57 14 84, at 6:30 pm—Assembly of the first degree. Initiation of:

• Wanzel Summer, chaplain at Erdberg

• Wolfgang A. Mozart, choirmaster.

Mozart received registration no. 20.

24

57 _____ 84

XII

[December 24, 5784/AD 1784]

The Proceedings of the Assembly of the Lodge "Charity" mentions the presence of Wolfgang A. Mozart.

7

57 _____ 85

I

[January 7, 5785/AD 1785]

Extract from the Proceedings of the Assembly of the Lodge "zur Wahren Eintracht" ("True Harmony"). 1° Opening of the Work for the Degree of Entered Apprentice and of Fellowcraft. The Brothers . . . as well as Brother Wolfgang A. Mozart, at the request of the honored Lodge "Charity" was raised to the second degree, following the usual ceremonial.

14

57 _____ 85

I

[January 14, 5785/AD 1785]

The Proceedings of the Assembly of the Lodge "True Harmony" makes mention of the presence of Wolfgang A. Mozart, "Member of the Honorable Lodge 'Charity.'"

28

57 _____ 85

I

[January 28, 5785/AD 1785]

The Proceedings of the Assembly of the Lodge "True Harmony" makes mention of the presence of Wolfgang A. Mozart, "Member of the Honorable Lodge 'Charity.'"

28 57 _____ 85 III	[March 28, 5785/AD 1785] Communication from the Honorable Lodge "Charity": Proposal for the initiation of the choirmaster, Leopold Mozart and Basky. The two postulants having to be absent for a trip, a dispensation was requested for this initiation to the 1st degree. The Secretary: Schwanckhardt.
March 29, 1785	The newspaper *Wienreal Zeitung* notes that one can find for sale at the Artaria gallery, three symphonies of J. Haydn (in A, in F, in D) as well as three concertos for piano by Mozart (in A, in F, in C) printed by the same publisher.
1 57 _____ 85 IV	[April 1, 5785/AD 1785] The Lodge "Charity" declares that it has received dispensation to proceed with the initiation of Leopold Mozart (he will be initiated on April 6).
16 57 _____ 85 IV	[April 16, 5785/AD 1785] Extract from the Proceedings of the Lodge "True Harmony": After the opening of the Lodge for the degrees of Entered Apprentice and Fellowcraft, the Brothers . . . and Leopold Mozart have, at their request, been elevated to the degree of Fellowcraft.
22 57 _____ 85 IV	[April 22, 5785/AD 1785] The Proceedings of the Lodge "True Harmony" mentions the presence of Visiting Brothers, in particular Leopold and Wolfgang Mozart, from the Lodge "Charity." [Author's note: On the registry, the signature of Leopold is crossed out since he did not have the right, being only Fellowcraft, to be present at the work of the Middle Chamber

(3rd degree); but this would suggest that Wolfgang, whose signature was not crossed out, was already Master at this date.] In addition, the Grand Master, at the request of the Grand Master of "Charity," proposes to elevate Leopold to the degree of Master, a ceremony that was later carried out.

12 57 _____ 85 VIII	[August 12, 5785/AD 1785] The Proceedings of the Lodge "True Harmony" mentions the presence of the Brother W. A. Mozart from the Lodge "Charity."
August 17, 1785	Artaria makes known the availability of the cantata "Mason's Joy," with piano accompaniment by the Choirmaster W. A. Mozart.
15 57 _____ 85 X	[October 15, 5785/AD 1785] The Lodges "Three Eagles" and "The Palm" invite the sister Lodges of Vienna to a concert given for the benefit of Visiting Brothers, players of the basset horn, Anton David d'Offenburg and Vincent Spingen from Prague. Also participating in this concert will be the Brothers Stadler and Mozart. The latter will perform an improvisation on the piano, always so appreciated by his Brothers. [Author's Note: After this meeting, it is interesting to remark that Mozart became interested in this instrument, which he used in future compositions.]
19 57 _____ 85 XII	[December 19, 5785/AD 1785] The Proceedings of the Lodge "True Harmony" mentions the presence of the Brother Wolfgang A. Mozart from the Lodge "Charity."

March 30, 1787   Mention of Mozart in the Golden Book of his Brother Johan Georg Kronauer: "Wisdom counts more than feelings."
Signed: Your true Brother and Friend W. A. Mozart, member of the Lodge "New Hope Crowned."

November 18, 1791   Consecration of a new Temple of the Lodge "New Hope Crowned."
On this occasion, Brother Wolfgang A. Mozart conducted a Masonic cantata composed November 15, 1791. (Extract from the newspaper *Der Heimliche Botschafter*.)

Notes

PREFACE

1. Carl de Nys, *La Musique religieuse de Mozart* (Paris: PUF Collection Que sais-je?, 1982), 100 and following pages.
2. De Nys, *La Musique religieuse de Mozart.*

1. MOZART, MASONIC BROTHER

1. Roger Cotte, *La Musique maçonnique et ses musiciens* (Braine-le-Comte, Belgium: Éditions du Baucens, 1975).
2. Jacques Chailley, *The Magic Flute Unveiled: Esoteric Symbolism in Mozart's Masonic Opera* (Rochester, Vt.: Inner Traditions, 1992), 68.
3. Howard C. Robbins Landon, *Mozart: The Golden Years, 1781–1791* (New York: Thames and Hudson, 2006), 111.
4. Robbins Landon, *Mozart: The Golden Years,* 104.

2. THE SYMBOLISM'S CONTENT

1. Cotte, *La Musique maçonnique,* 105.
2. Alfred Einstein, *Mozart: His Character, His Work* (Oxford: Oxford University Press, 1945), 104.
3. Jean and Brigitte Massin, *Wolfgang Amadeus Mozart* (Paris: Éditions Fayard, 1970).
4. Teodor de Wyzewa and Georges de Saint-Foix, *W. A. Mozart: Sa vie musicale et son oeuvre* (Paris: Éditions Desclée et Brouwer, 2 vols., 1977–1978).

Notes

3. From Symbols to Music

1. Rémy Stricker, *Mozart et ses Opéras: Fiction et vérité* [Mozart and His Operas: Fiction and Truth] (Paris: Éditions Gallimard, 1980), 317.
2. Chailley, *The Magic Flute Unveiled*, 170.
3. Philippe Alexandre Autexier, *Les Oeuvres témoins de Mozart* [The Initial Works of Mozart] (Paris: Éditions Alphonse Leduc, 1982), 42.
4. Ibid., 43.
5. Chailley, *The Magic Flute Unveiled*, 171, 172.
6. Michel Tamisier, *Mozart, Hölderin: suivi de Don Juan ou le myth du théâtre* [Mozart, Hölderlin: Follow-up to Don Juan or The Myth of Theater] (Paris: Éditions La Délirante, 1975).

4. Brief Works for Special Occasions in Masonic Assemblies

1. Roger Cotte, *La Musique maçonnique*, 100.

5. Works of a Masonic Character That Are Not Ritualistic

1. De Wyzewa and St-Foix, *W. A. Mozart: Sa vie musicale*.
2. Einstein, *Mozart*, 422

6. First Period: 1785

1. Cuthbert Girdlestone, *Mozart and His Piano Concertos* (New York: Dover Publications, 1964), 309.
2. Jean-Victor Hocquard, *Mozart, L'amour, la mort* [Mozart: The Love, the Death] (Paris: Garamont-Archimbaud, 1987).
3. Girdlestone, *Mozart and His Piano Concertos*, 313.

8. Third Period: 1791

1. Autexier, *Les Oeuvres témoins de Mozart*, 95 and following pages.

9. Wolfgang's Legacy

1. Tubeuf: 1990 catalog for the Aix Festival, 51.
2. Ibid.

Bibliography

Autexier, Philippe A. *Mozart*. Paris: Champion, 1987.

———. *Les Oeuvres témoins de Mozart* [The Initial Works of Mozart]. Paris: Alphonse Leduc, 1982.

Einstein, Alfred. *Mozart: His Character, His Work*. New York: Oxford University Press, 1945.

Chailley, Jacques. *The Magic Flute Unveiled: Esoteric Symbolism in Mozart's Masonic Opera*. Rochester, Vt.: Inner Traditions, 1992.

Girdlestone, Cuthbert. *Mozart and His Piano Concertos*. New York: Dover, 1964.

Grande Loge de France. "Mozart Franc-Maçon" [Mozart Freemason]. *Les cahiers pour la célébration du bicentenaire de la naissance, Bulletin intérieur,* no. 36, January 1956.

Hutin, Serge. *Les Francs-Maçons* [The Freemasons]. Paris: Éditions du Seuil, 1960.

Hocquard, Jean-Victor. *Mozart, L'amour, la mort* [Mozart: The Love, the Death]. Paris: Garamont-Archimbaud, 1987.

Hutchings, Arthur. *Mozart: The Man, the Musician*. New York: Schirmer Books, 1976.

Robbins Landon, H. C. *1791: Mozart's Last Year*. New York: Schirmer Books, 1988.

———. *Mozart: The Golden Years, 1781–1791*. New York: Thames and Hudson, 2006.

Massin, Jean, and Brigitte Massin. *Wolfgang Amadeus Mozart*. Paris: Fayard, 1970.

Nettl, Paul. *Mozart and Masonry*. New York: Dorset, 1957.

Niemetschek, Franz Xaver. *Mozart: The First Biography*. New York: Berghahn Books, 2006.

De Nys, Carl. *La Musique religieuse de Mozart* [The Religious Music of Mozart]. Paris: PUF Collection Que sais-je?, 1982.

————. *Mozart et Dieu* [Mozart and God]. Collection Génies et réalités. Paris: Hachette, 1984.

Roussel, Paul. *Mozart Seen Through 50 Masterpieces.* Montreal: Habitex Books, 1976.

Stricker, Rémy. *Mozart et ses opéras: Fiction et vérité* [Mozart and His Operas: Fiction and Truth]. Paris: Gallimard, 1980.

Tamisier, Michel. *Mozart, Hölderlin: suivi de Don Juan ou le mythe du théâtre* [Mozart, Hölderlin: Follow-up to Don Juan or The Myth of Theater]. Paris: Délirante, 1975.

De Wyzewa, Teodor, and Georges de Saint-Foiz. *W. A. Mozart: Sa vie musicale et son oeuvre* [W. A. Mozart: His Musical Life and His Work]. 2 volumes. Paris: Desclée de Brouwer, 1977–1978.

Index
of Cited Works

Index

BOOKS OF RELATED INTEREST

THE MAGIC FLUTE UNVEILED
Esoteric Symbolism in Mozart's Masonic Opera
by Jacques Chailley

HARMONIES OF HEAVEN AND EARTH
Mysticism in Music from Antiquity to the Avant-Garde
by Joscelyn Godwin

THE HARMONY OF THE SPHERES
The Pythagorean Tradition in Music
by Joscelyn Godwin

THE SECRET LORE OF MUSIC
The Hidden Power of Orpheus
by Fabre d'Olivet
Translated by Joscelyn Godwin

THE SPIRITUAL DIMENSIONS OF MUSIC
Altering Consciousness for Inner Development
by R. J. Stewart

FOUNDING FATHERS, SECRET SOCIETIES
Freemasons, Illuminati, Rosicrucians,
and the Decoding of the Great Seal
by Robert Hieronimus, Ph.D. with Laura Cortner

THE SECRET HISTORY OF FREEMASONRY
Its Origins and Connection to the Knights Templar
by Paul Naudon

THE MAGUS OF FREEMASONRY
The Mysterious Life of Elias Ashmole—Scientist, Alchemist,
and Founder of the Royal Society
by Tobias Churton

Inner Traditions • Bear & Company
P.O. Box 388
Rochester, VT 05767
1-800-246-8648
www.InnerTraditions.com

Or contact your local bookseller